OUTLAWS
OF THE CANADIAN WEST

LONE PINE

M.A. Macphe

The Publisher: Lone Pine Publishing

10145-81 Ave.   1901 Raymond Ave. SW, Suite C
Edmonton, AB T6E 1W9   Renton, WA 98055
Canada   USA

Canadian Cataloguing in Publication Data

Macpherson, M.A.
    Outlaws of the Canadian west
    ISBN 1-55105-166-4

    1. Outlaw—Canada, Western—Biography. 2. Criminals—Canada,
Western—Biography. 3. Crime—Canada, Western—History. I. Title.
HV6805.M32 1999   364.1'092'2712   C99-911030-6

Editorial Director: Nancy Foulds
Project Editor: Eloise Pulos
Editorial: Eloise Pulos, Lee Craig
Production Manager: Jody Reekie
Cover Design: Rob Weidemann
Book Design: Heather Markham
Layout & Production: Heather Markham, Monica Triska
Maps: Ian Sheldon
Scanning: Elite Lithographers

Cover Photographs: Billy Miner, courtesy B.C. Archives; Gun of Almighty Voice and Ernest Cashel (back cover) courtesy Glenbow Archives, Calgary, Canada; 1880s train, courtesy Kelowna Centennial Museum; old building in Bannack, MT, courtesy Dolores Steele.

Photographs were supplied with the kind permission of the following:
B.C. Archives (p. 10, A-04098; p. 26, D-07224; p. 68, G-06831; p. 71, A-01459, A-01456; p. 82, ZZ-95124; p. 144, A-01617; p. 153, B-03244; p. 154, B-02860; p. 156, C-05792; p. 159, C-05793; p. 164–165, A-03483; p. 168, C-05482; p. 171, D-07222; p. 180, A-07788); Glenbow Archives, Calgary, Canada (p. 20, NA-674-49; pp. 34–35, NA-550-18; p. 54, NA-504-1; pp. 64–65, NA-504-2; p. 104, NA-118-54; pp. 116–117, NA-670-7; p. 118, NA-2310-1; p. 129, NA-1811-26; p. 130, NA-452-2; p. 135, NA-2172-36; p. 137, NA-1644-161; p. 194, NA-1136-1; p. 205, NA-2899-10; p. 213, NA-3282-2; p. 216, NA-1258-119; p. 223, NA-1685-1; p. 229, NA-1258-102); Provincial Archives of Manitoba (pp. 46–47, The main street of Winnipeg, c. 1873, N971); Nanaimo District Museum (pp. 176–177); New Westminster Museum/Archives (pp. 80–81); Prince Rupert City & Regional Archives (pp. 182–183, L984-39-1881); Saskatchewan Archives Board (p. 94, R-B7353).

We acknowledge the financial support of the Government of Canada through the Book Publishing Industry Development Program (BPIDP) for our publishing activities.

PC: P6   Canada

CONTENTS

Dedication: For Craig

FOREWORD

The world of these unsavoury characters from the past was vastly different from today's world. A hundred years ago or more, the West was scattered with groups of First Nations peoples and small settlements of fur traders, farmers and entrepreneurs. There were no telephones, fax machines or e-mail; when you wanted to talk to someone some distance away you wrote a letter or sent a telegram. Transportation was by foot, horse, cart, stagecoach or train; there were no cars, subways, airplanes or freeways. In the world of crime investigation, there was no DNA analysis; fingerprinting didn't become common in crime detection until the early twentieth century and criminals were dispatched at the end of a rope.

The Canadian West was called Rupert's Land and was under the firm control of fur traders who eventually amalgamated under the Hudson's Bay Company, which had possessed and exploited the vast territory draining into Hudson Bay since 1670. Settlers began accumulating after the Earl of Selkirk established the Red River Colony in 1812. Decades passed and in the 1850s John Palliser and his expedition travelled across the region to assess its potential for agriculture. The Dominion of Canada was formed in 1867 and two years later it purchased Rupert's Land and planned for a massive wave of settlement to the virtually unoccupied land on much the same scale as was occurring south of the border, where homesteads were being taken up in large numbers.

Settlement occurred much slower than was anticipated, however, partly because there was still more attractive land available in the States and partly because of economic downturns worldwide. Manitoba was formed in 1870 after the Riel Rebellion prompted a bit more notice on the part of the eastern politicians. Other conflicts such as the Cypress Hills Massacre in 1873 and fears of a take-over from the south prompted eastern politicians to again bend their attention to the West. Proper policing was the answer, they decided, so the North-West Mounted Police was formed and marched west in 1874. The illegal trade in whiskey to the native peoples came under scrutiny and the key traders either departed abruptly or turned to operations that fell on the sunny side of the law.

Through the 1870s treaties were negotiated with the Indian nations of the West. During that decade, huge herds of buffalo, long the mainstay of almost every aspect of native life, were obliterated from the prairies and a way of life ended abruptly as disease, starvation, alcoholism and destitution set in. The expectation from the East was that the native nations, which had occupied the area for tens of centuries, would quietly but quickly slip onto small, scattered reserves and take up agriculture and the white man's ways, leaving the bulk of the land to "civilization."

Meanwhile, out on the Coast, Governor Douglas selected the site for Fort Victoria in 1843. Things began to cook after the Fraser River Gold Rush began in 1858, bringing herds of miners and all their hangers-on—all the way from bakers and bankers to belles of the evening—into the fur-trade community. Vancouver, on the mainland, was somewhat slower to develop in the 1860s as the Cariboo Gold Rush in the Interior began to pick up speed. The Canadian Pacific Railway boosted the local economy right off the bat when it decided to take advantage of a better harbour there instead of at Port Moody, previously the proposed terminus of the transcontinental line built in the 1880s. The native groups in what became the province of British Columbia were expected to move to reserves away from the mainstream settlements and they were to encounter many of the same hardships as their counterparts on the plains.

In the North, settlements were scarcer and farther apart. After the Klondike Gold Rush in the Yukon dwindled a few years after the twentieth century dawned, small populations of whites remained amid scattered groups of native peoples. The North-West Mounted Police figured strongly in this remote area too, where distances and weather conditions often made their official efforts more arduous. The force was re-named the Royal North-West Mounted Police in 1904 and joined the Dominion Police in 1920 to form the Royal Canadian Mounted Police.

By the 1930s, when the Great Depression seized the land, electricity, airplanes, telephones, typewriters, fingerprinting and automobiles had made their mark on everyday life and on the criminal element. Canada celebrated its fiftieth birthday in

1927, and by then the provinces of Alberta and Saskatchewan had been formed and towns and cities had sprung up across the West. Times had changed.

Over the nine or so decades from the 1850s to the 1930s, seventeen or so characters stand head and shoulders above the other common criminals of their times. There was usually a killing, sometimes of a police officer but not always, plus some kind of chase in which the bad guys were on the lam for months and sometimes years whilst the police attempted to track them down, then a final shoot-out or seminal event that resulted in justice. In all but a couple of cases, the bottom line was always the same: they ended up at the noose end of a rope or the wrong end of a fast bullet. Despite the overwhelming lack of today's technological advantages—efficient transportation, communication and criminal investigation just as a start—the police managed to capture the bad guys and bring them to justice. It just took longer and involved more travel.

We've organized the bad guys by decade. Sometimes the bulk of the crimes occurred in the decade before the criminals' fate was sealed, but it's a loose enough structure to accommodate longer-running activities. We start in the 1850s in Victoria with the colourful One-Ear Charles Brown, a bootlegger and cop-killer who met his end vigilante-style across the line in 1867. In the 1860s, Boon Helm, a murderer and cannibal from the western U.S., graced the gold-fields of British Columbia and picked off a few gold-miners before meeting his end in the gallows.

The 1870s saw a ragtag group of whiskey traders at Fort Whoop-Up and an equally disreputable band of wolfers in the Cypress Hills set in motion the creation of the North-West Mounted Police. In 1870 the Manitoba Provincial

Police was formed and in 1874, twenty-three-year-old Richard Power was appointed Manitoba's Chief Constable. Packing a mighty .45 Colt revolver, Power gave ten of the best years of his life fighting crime, before meeting an untimely death during an arrest. Near Fort Saskatchewan, in what is now Alberta, late in the decade, Swift Runner ran amok, eventually to kill and consume his entire family, mother included.

The 1880s began with four hangings: the wild McLean Gang of the Nicola Valley in the Interior of British Columbia terrorized and murdered until the long arm of the law caught up with them. Also in the 1880s, Bulldog Kelly's murder of a liquor salesman in the B.C. Interior almost resulted in an international incident after his escape into the U.S. prompted an unsuccessful extradition attempt. About the same time, Racette and Gaddy, ex-con horsethieves and thinkers, arranged the professional photograph of themselves that later was used on the wanted poster produced after they killed a rancher near Wolsely, Saskatchewan.

The century turned with young Ernest Cashel, who recommended, "Don't do anything boys you are afraid to let your mother know" and was hanged in Calgary after killing a settler. Farther west in the Interior of B.C., the charming Grey Fox, Billy Miner the Gentleman Bandit, became a hero by robbing the Canadian Pacific Railway enough times to endear him to locals who were tired of being crushed under the weight of the eastern-based corporation.

A few years later, in the 1910s, Paul Spintlum and Moses Paul bludgeoned a man to death and then escaped into the woods, pursued by the Mounties in a chase that lasted two years and left five dead. Some time later, out on Vancouver Island, Flying Dutchman Henry Wagner's robbing spree ended in a final wrestling match following a cop-killing. Meanwhile, the on-again off-again thirteen-year pursuit of Simon Gun-an-noot was underway, the upshot of which was a capture and an innocent verdict.

In the late teens and early 1920s, a bootlegger and his belle managed to buy a date with a hangman after one of them killed a cop in the Crowsnest. In the early 1930s, with the Depression casting a pall throughout the country, the Mad Trapper's murder of a policeman resulted in a months-long arctic chase in the depths of winter.

There's lots of materials on these bad guys. Put your feet up and read on.

FORT VICTORIA

1

ONE-EAR CHARLES BROWN: A VIGILANTE KILLING WINS APPLAUSE

...for notorious bad-boy Charles H. Brown, the coastal community of Victoria provided fertile ground.

Schemers and dreamers were a dime a dozen in the busy port town of Victoria in the mid-1800s when ships hauling lumber and coal were as plentiful as the swirling promises of a fortune in gold to be had somewhere inside the fierce Interior.

Gold on the Fraser, gold in the Cariboo, gold in the East Kootenays—these were the cries in the hills of what is now British Columbia at a time when fortune seekers and swindlers, miners and mutineers existed together in a brave New World forged out of wilderness.

But for notorious bad-boy Charles H. Brown, the coastal community of Victoria provided fertile ground for another type of trade, that of liquid gold. Brown was not the only bootlegger arrested around the Hudson's Bay post of Fort Victoria in the late 1850s and early 1860s, but he was one of Vancouver Island's most distasteful traders. He was a man who thought nothing of claiming barrels of seawater were whiskey, and then selling them at an inflated price to unsuspecting natives.

It's no surprise then, that Charlie Brown was one of a handful of men living outside the law who died outside the law. He was eventually hunted down and killed by vigilantes who thought that due justice for the likes of characters such as Brown couldn't wait for the pomp and circumstance of a formal courtroom and came best from the barrel of a smoking gun.

Very little is to be discovered about his early days, but from all reports it seems Brown was a born thug from the western U.S. who drifted up to Canada to avoid confrontation with marshals on the other side of the line. He set himself up as a bootlegger on the outskirts of the settlement of Victoria in the 1850s but wasn't identified by police as a ne'er-do-well until his first arrest in 1859.

Brown had been selling whiskey laced with lamp oil to natives in the villages around the harbour and was caught after cadging twenty dollars from a native man with a promise of alcohol and then not delivering the goods.

The constabulary who knocked on the door of Brown's shack found a surly, thick-set man with no respect for the law or the rights of others. Unable to find Brown's still or source of whiskey, the police kept his shack under surveillance until Sergeant A.S. Blake caught Brown in the process of selling a ten-gallon can of firewater to a native man from a northern tribe.

Brown was arrested and brought to court on charges of selling alcohol to Indians, an offence in the Crown Colony, but he was let off with a stern warning and a small fine. Little did the police know, their relationship with Charlie Brown, who would go down in the history of British Columbia as the notorious murderer One-Ear Brown, was just in its infancy.

In April 1861 Brown was again in front of the Bastion Square Court of Justice on charges of bootlegging and endangering an officer. He and an accomplice, a man named John Guest, had driven a wagon full of whiskey barrels onto the Songhees reserve, southwest of the settlement. With police observing from the cover of the dense woods, the men unloaded the contraband liquor at a planned rendezvous site. There was an exchange of money between Brown and the company of three or four natives who had met the clandestine wagon.

As Brown and Guest were driving away, Victoria Police Superintendent William Smith jumped on the empty wagon and confronted Brown with his bootlegging practice. Gazing down the muzzle of a revolver, Brown must have decided surrender was wisest. He and one of the natives, subdued by Sergeant Blake, were brought back to town and taken directly to prison. As they were being led into the lock-up, a Queen Charlotte Indian Chief named Eden-sah, rushed by the sentry posted at the prison gates and fired a shot at Blake with a large dragoon pistol. Fortunately for the officer, the bullet missed its intended mark, and Eden-sah was quickly wrestled to the ground, subdued and also arrested.

The attempted murder charge against Eden-sah delayed Brown's own court appearance but Justices Pemberton, de Courcy and Brew, presiding in the Victoria courthouse, must have seen the link between the two crimes. Despite a guilty plea on the part of Brown, and a heartfelt appeal for mercy on his behalf by defence council D.B. Ring, the judges felt a lesson needed to be learned. Because most of the crimes involving natives were linked to alcohol consumption, those selling or, as Justice de Courcy put it, "putting liquor in the way of Indians," would suffer dire consequences.

Charlie Brown was sentenced to a year of hard labour in the chain gang, repairing settlement streets shackled to other offenders in a crude work party. It was either that or pay a $500 fine. Somehow, likely through an unsolved theft, the bootlegging bounder chose the latter. He coughed up the money but buying his freedom wouldn't buy him time away from the law.

Three months later, Brown was back in court on charges of assault and bootlegging. He'd continued to ply his trade but was accosted by a Haida native with the unlikely name of Captain Jefferson, who claimed Brown had sold his tribe salt-water instead of whiskey from the deck of the schooner *Laurel*. A scuffle ensued and the Haida was severely beaten, enough so that he went to police with his woesome tale.

The authorities in Victoria were, by this point, sick to death of Charlie Brown and his wretched lifestyle. They sentenced him to six months with the chain gang and, with six pounds of iron manacled to his ankle, Brown shuffled through Victoria picking horse dung off the streets and repairing wooden sidewalks. Some strange superstition made him refuse to tend the settlement's cemetery, and, as punishment, was put behind bars in the gloomy central Bastion Square Jail and fed only bread and water.

It was there that Charlie Brown won his infamous nickname. In a bid for freedom, the contemptuous Brown jumped on the back of guard Edward Wright in an effort to wrestle away his pistol. Wright managed to pull his revolver in time and in the struggle it went off, blasting Brown's right ear from the side of his head. The sudden shot and the sharp pain of the cartilage being severed from his skull brought Brown to his senses. Shrieking with pain, blood pumping from the wound, he surrendered all thoughts of freedom. The prison would remain the bootlegger's home and, in fact, Judge Pemberton added a year to his sentence for his attempted escape. Despite his best efforts, however, One-Ear Charlie, as he was now known, only served three months of the additional sentence.

Feigning illness, Brown finally escaped custody from the Victoria Hospital in July 1862. After Charlie'd been on the lam for ten days, a journalist for the *Victoria Colonist* made mention of the futile search by lawmen noting "[Brown is]...a very troublesome customer and if he never returns, the colony is fortunate to get rid of his presence so cheaply."

Leaving the Island precipitated not only a change of venue for Brown's outlaw activities, it also prompted a change of career. He headed for the Interior cattle country, and spent the next five years developing skills as a horse thief and cattle rustler between Idaho, Montana and the wide-open timber country of northern British Columbia.

It was likely the news of a new gold source, the recently discovered Stud Horse Creek, that lured One-Ear Charlie Brown to the East Kootenays in 1867. By the time One-Ear Charlie got to the Stud Horse, between 5000 and 8000 men had gathered some 600 miles east of Victoria, hoping to siphon into their own pockets some of the gold dust of the creek's yield, an average of $76,000 a day.

Brown's unquenchable hunger for cash certainly led him to the district but, quite unwittingly, he was also leading two Idaho Dutchmen to the wild camp that had sprung up near the Kootenay River. They were pursuing Brown on horseback, trailing him since the spring when he'd stolen three horses from their ranch. While Brown didn't know it, the two Americans were bound and determined to get their horses back and teach the brazen thief a lesson.

Tracking One-Ear to his camp, the Dutchmen decided to enlist the assistance of local police officers living in the Stud Horse (also known as Wild Horse) Creek community. Three police officers, James Normansell, John Carrington and rookie Jack Lawson, were stationed at the boomtown to remind gold-frenzied miners that law and order needed to prevail on the frontier. The two veteran officers were on patrol but the young officer, Lawson, agreed to help the Dutchmen find their horses. It was a decision that would cost him his life.

On July 18, 1867, short days after the birth of the Dominion of Canada on July 1, Lawson and the two unnamed Idaho ranchers rode into Brown's camp. Lawson led the way, and as he saw Brown coming towards him on the trail, he asked the bootlegger about the stolen ponies. Brown reached for his pistol at the same moment Lawson drew his gun.

"Don't move, cowboy," said the lawman, indicating Brown should raise his hands in the air. He turned to speak to the men, but before the words were out of his mouth, One-Ear let out a shot that took the back off the officer's head. Lawson's horse reared and Lawson spun from the saddle, landing heavily on the ground. He was dead.

The Dutchmen turned tail and galloped off quickly to Stud Horse Creek, alerting authorities of the murder but, because the senior officers weren't available, justice fell into the hands of grim civilians. Four implacable miners took to the saddle, now intent on making One-Ear Charlie Brown pay for his violent crime.

Brown, too, had fled as soon as Lawson fell. He knew he'd have to make it to the border if he was going to avoid hanging, the standard punishment for killing an officer of law on British territory. So with a desperadoe's desperation he headed south for Idaho, a pack of enraged miners, the vigilante committee, hot on his heels.

Mere hours behind the fugitive, the posse reached the swollen St. Mary's River learning that Brown had commandeered a raft that had been swamped in rough water. It seemed he had lost all his supplies, for at the next camp, that of miner Joe Davis, they were told One-Ear Charlie had been there begging for ammunition.

The posse pressed on, ever gaining ground on their prey. About twelve miles south of Davis' camp, they came upon a Chinese man who reiterated the same story: a desperate man, mutilated about the face and seemingly frantic for supplies, had demanded ammunition and weapons but, he insisted, none had been provided. It seemed One-Ear Charlie Brown's gig was just about up. The thundering hooves of the posse must have drummed in his one good ear as he crossed the border into the States.

Where Bonner's Ferry crosses the Kootenay River south of the border, the posse stopped and lay in wait for the bandit. They had been informed that Brown was now behind them, travelling on foot, and he was bound to come their way. It was now just a matter of time.

An hour later, flies were landing on the bloodied carcass of One-Ear Charlie Brown. The miners had seen him advancing, and as though by pre-planned signal, each raised his double-barrelled shotgun and blasted the fugitive into eternity. With their task completed, the satisfied miners of Stud Horse Creek let the body lie where it fell, beside the Walla Walla trail. The next morning, July 20, 1867, they returned to the site to put One-Ear Charlie Brown, police murderer and bootlegger, into a shallow grave.

Vigilante killings certainly weren't encouraged in the colony but, British rule aside, no one lamented Charlie Brown's execution. A newspaper editorial appeared in the *New Westminster British Columbian* as follows:

"As a rule, we are not an admirer of Vigilante Committees.... The Kootenay case seems to have been a terrible affair.... "That the constable of the district was shot and killed is undoubtedly correct. Ardent believers in law and order may deprecate the infliction of summary punishment by an unauthorized body; wretched Brown showed the course they adopted a proper and just appreciation of the law. ...

"Clearly with the representatives of the law and the power of the Government lying dead before them, the right, the duty of the people was to prevent the flight of the evildoer. They had to choose between the escape of the murderer and his summary punishment. Aware that he was guilty of a capital offence in the eyes of the law, and well knowing that if he crossed the line he was safe from pursuit [the newspaper obviously thought the One-Ear's death occurred on Canadian soil], they decided to shoot him down.

"Paradoxical as the assertion may appear, when the miners took the law into their own hands and executed the criminal, they showed a high appreciation of the law and upheld its majesty."

So, a crew of angry miners avenged the death of a lawman by taking justice into their own hands. They left bootlegger-turned-murderer One-Ear Charlie Brown dead on the American side of the Forty-ninth Parallel. No one wept.

WILLIAMS CREEK IN THE CARIBOO GOLD-FIELDS

2

BOONE HELM: A MONSTER DISGUISED AS A HUMAN

...buried gold has a story to tell...a tale of murder and cannibalism by one of the West's most heinous criminals.

Cariboo country in north-central British Columbia has long been a beacon for gold-hungry men. In the 1860s, creeks laden with gold drew men to the Cariboo gold rush. Today, a rumoured stash of gold dust worth over one million dollars draws treasure hunters into the area near Quesnel.

The buried gold has a story to tell and it's a tale of murder and cannibalism by one of the West's most heinous criminals, Boone Helm. He is the one who buried the stolen gold under a particular cedar tree on a trail that leads north to the gold dredges of Antler Creek. And he brutally murdered three men to get their hard-won earnings. The saddle bags stuffed with raw gold are still there somewhere, because Boone Helm was strung up in the States before he could get back to his booty. The gold is tainted with blood—not the first blood to be spilled in Cariboo country but certainly spilled by one of its most infamous occupants.

Born in Kentucky around 1828, Boone was the second youngest of five brothers, all of whom had died violently. He was raised in a household where holding your own meant striking out with your fists and if a weapon was handy, all the better. Reports of his early days in and around Monroe County, Missouri, tell of an illiterate braggart who never went anywhere without a weapon. Helm was an excellent knife thrower and would sooner toss a blade into a man who walked across his shadow than veer slightly off course.

Boone Helm's first murder was in Jefferson City, Wyoming, and like most of the murders that followed this black-hearted being, it involved the senseless slaughter of an unsuspecting friend. When potential travel companion Littlebury Shoot wouldn't agree to strike out with him for California, Boone put an end to the argument by plunging his knife into Shoot's heart. Shoot died instantly and Helm, as though it made not a whit of difference whether Shoot was dead or alive, lit off for the California gold-fields. At the age of twenty-four, he was already wanted for murder.

Captured in a native camp and returned to Missouri, Helm feigned insanity and was locked up in an asylum rather than a prison. Probably because he was reported to be a nice-looking man, Helm must have had almost a split personality. Like a chameleon, he transformed himself into the model patient, charming the doctors and guards, until he saw an opportunity to escape. Once over the walls of the asylum, Boone Helm reverted to his horrible self again, and carried on to California, murdering several people along the way. He always claimed he killed to defend himself, but in 1858, a gunshot in the back of a fleeing victim destroyed the self-defence theory and Helm found himself wanted for murder in the State of California.

Fleeing to The Dalles, Oregon, to save himself from certain lynching, Helm got wind of the gold discovery on the Fraser River in a far northern territory, the Crown Colonies of Vancouver Island and British Columbia. But gold was even closer at hand. A party of gambling prospectors had decided to set out for Camp Floyd, Utah, some fifty miles southwest of Salt Lake City, where another gold strike was rumoured. Helm, who had no desire to work for gold but realized it was there for the taking for anyone with guns and guts, hastened to join the group in their trek across 500 miles of hostile Indian lands.

One of the men in the group, Elijah Burton, was a notorious gambler. He was convinced the roulette wheel and a couple of packs of marked cards would win him a fortune as easily as Helm was convinced his loaded pistols would do the job. Together with three others, they trudged across rough terrain until attacked by Indians at their camp on the shores of the Bannock River. One of the party was killed by a stray arrow but, with the weather closing in and the tops of the mountains already covered in snow, the four remaining men decided to carry on to Camp Floyd. It was a poorly thought-out decision. By November, winter had truly set in, and the group had only started to pack through the Wasatch Mountain Range.

The men struck camp in the mountains and decided it was best to stay in one place rather than brave the elements. They proceeded to kill and eat their horses as the only way to keep death by starvation at bay. Helm had another way to avoid hunger tucked away in the back of his diabolical mind, however, and Elijah Burton ended up on the losing side of a life gamble when he agreed to leave the camp with Helm to see if they could make it through the mountains.

There is evidence the two men eventually reached their destination in the wickedly cold winter of 1859, but the post was found abandoned. In desperation Helm murdered, then butchered his gambling companion, eating large chunks of the man's flesh.

Thus sustained, Helm carried on towards Salt Lake City. His crime would likely have gone undiscovered save for a chance encounter on the trail with a starving Indian. In what may have been his only gracious act, Helm unwrapped a package he was hauling on his back and offered the horrified man a portion of Burton's leg. The native declined the human flesh but reportedly watched Helm gnaw at the meat around the upper calf. It was an unsavoury sight.

Almost eight months after leaving The Dalles, Helm arrived in Salt Lake City. He had robbed Burton before killing him and used the man's $1400 of gold dust to survive in the city. When the money ran out, Helm turned to his usual means, stealing horses, robbing people and as always, committing murder. In a botched pony-thieving expedition in 1861, he killed two men who had been guarding a corral of horses. When a soldier from the U.S. Army quartermaster corps recognized him, Helm put a bullet through his head in a crowded saloon in Lodi, Utah.

After that killing and a quick escape across state lines, Helm drifted to California and later resurfaced in Washington Territory where he killed again. It was the death of Dutch Fred, a well-known gambler, that finally forced the murdering cannibal over the line into Canada. With the same nonchalance displayed in the first killing of his friend Littlebury Shoot, Helm fired point-blank into Dutch Fred's back as he sat unarmed at a gambling table. An argument prompted the killing, but Dutch Fred had too many friends to let his murder go unavenged. A gang set on vigilante justice pursued Boone Helm to the state line and left him only when he disappeared into British Columbia's wilderness.

The option to flee to Canada wasn't totally random for the man who had terrorized the Pacific Northwest for almost twenty years. In the same way word had reached him of the 1858 Fraser River gold rush, the words Cariboo country and "rivers of gold" were now on everyone's lips. "Quick money for the killing" might be the phrase that sprang to mind as he landed in the City of Victoria on Vancouver Island, October 12, 1862. But Helm had a few lessons to learn in the process of law and order, lessons he had somehow avoided in the rough-and-tumble world of an outlaw living south of the border. In this part of North America no one was above the rules. Boone Helm, who thought nothing of killing and eating a friend, had a lot to learn on foreign land.

His first run-in with police came mere hours after he'd disembarked from the steamer at Enterprise wharf in Victoria Harbour. He was imprisoned for the first time ever, over a minor incident: stealing apples and refusing to pay for drinks in Victoria's local public house, the downtown Adelphi Saloon. Justice, a cold prison cell and a courtroom trial were all new experiences for the murdering Helm. Like he did back in Missouri when imprisoned in the insane asylum, Helm put on his "poor, poor me" chameleon act in front of Judge Augustus Pemberton and his lawyer Mr. Bishop.

"I'm a stranger in a strange land," said the lanky, dark-hair Helm with downcast eyes. "If it weren't for the prison cell I occupied last night, I would have had to walk the streets of this fair city as I am wholly alone, penniless and afraid, having neither chick nor child, kith nor kin."

If it hadn't been for his boasting the night previous—including loud details of killing Dutch Fred—Pemberton might have bought into Helm's tale of woe. Suspecting they had unwittingly captured a American criminal wanted on murder charges, the judge gave an unusually tough penalty by way of keeping Helm behind bars until extradition proceedings could begin. Helm was sentenced to one month in prison or post a bond of more than $400. Out of necessity, he chose the former.

Unfortunately for his next string of victims, Helm served his time and was released from Victoria's Bastion Square Jail three days before the U.S. sheriff in Florence contacted Victoria's Police Chief Horace Smith. The order was to hold Helm until American authorities could come and get him, but by this time

Old Jail, Bastion Square, Victoria

Boone Helm had shaken the dust of Victoria off his feet. Helm was headed to the wilder Interior where justice was far less stringent and much more to his liking.

The Cariboo was booming and lawlessness abounded. It was the perfect breeding ground for murderous deeds, and Boone Helm wasn't in the area long before three miners, laden with gold, presented themselves to him as easy prey.

On July 18, 1862, two unnamed French Canadians and a man named Sokoloski were coming down from the mines near Williams Creek through to the Forks of Quesnelle, where the Quesnel River branches north and south. The Forks was the largest community in the Interior at the time and men often gravitated there for free-flowing whiskey and the favours of working women.

William Collinson was walking with the miners when they came down the forty-mile trail, but decided to forge ahead with his comrade Tommy Harvey when the Frenchmen and Sokoloski stopped at Keithley Creek for a bite to eat. It was the last time he saw the three men.

Collinson testified to seeing Helm some three miles outside of the Forks on his way into town but it wasn't until the next day, when he watched the bodies of the men being brought into town on stretchers, that he put the two incidents together. The miners were carrying $32,000—now worth $1 million—in coarse gold. Each man had a six-shooter devoid of shells and a bullet between the ears. The money was, of course, missing.

The murders evoked an immediate response of anger from the citizens of the Forks. They all suspected Boone Helm was responsible for the triple murders but no one had witnessed the crime. Nevertheless, a hasty meeting was convened and Helm was handed down a verdict of willful murder. Unfortunately, by the time a posse was organized, he had long since disappeared.

In May 1863, Boone Helm was apprehended in Fort Yale on the Fraser River on charges of murder. He had been attempting to cross the line back into the safe haven of the States. Hauled back to prison in Victoria, he was again held in the Bastion Square Jail until released into the hands of a special officer of the U.S. police force. Helm stood trial for the murder of Dutch Fred in Florence, Idaho, but after some wheeling and dealing by Helm's older brother, Tex, justice was thwarted yet again. By bribing a witness, Tex managed to weaken the prosecution's case so badly that his little brother walked out of the court-house a free man.

With Helm safely back in the States, B.C. police had no way to bring him back to Victoria to face trial for killing the Cariboo miners. But neither could Helm get his hands on the buried gold dust outside the Forks of Quesnelle. He linked up with the infamous Henry Plummer gang of Virginia City, Montana Territory, and as one of fifty hardened criminals continued a life of crime and violence.

A group of vigilantes from Virginia City finally did Canada a favour by nabbing five key members of the gang who called themselves, ironically, "The Innocents." Boone Helm was among the five, and it was in an unfinished log cabin, its wooden ridge pole open to the air, the murdering cannibal of the Cariboo would die by the noose.

On the morning of January 14, 1864, more than 5000 residents of Virginia City came out to watch the hanging of the five prisoners. Boone Helm, who had killed upwards of nine men, was led handcuffed to a three-foot packing crate that sat below the third noose. He was literally among a pack of other thieves: Jack Gallagher, murderer; Clubfoot Lane, horse thief and stagecoach robber; Frank Parrish, triple murderer, and Hayer Lyons, convicted of a double murder. Boone Helm, however, gained the dubious distinction of being named by his fellow gang members as "the most hardened, cool and deliberate scoundrel of the whole band." Up until the very end, Helm still tried to talk his way out of the hangman's rope.

"I am as innocent as the babe unborn," he is quoted as saying on the day of the execution, "…I am willing to swear it on the Bible." A Holy Bible was duly produced and without batting an eye, Helm swore before the crowd that he was innocent. In a flourish that caused the crowd to gasp in disbelief, the cannibal bent over and kissed the book.

When Jack Gallagher, lieutenant of the Plummer gang, had his packing crate kicked away, Helm shouted to the twitching body: "Kick away old fellow, I'll be in Hell with you in a minute."

With that, Helm leaped off his own box and fell to a dramatic and almost instantaneous death. The murdered men of the Cariboo, the chopped-up and consumed gambler of Utah and countless innocent others who fell to Boone Helm's hand, at last, had their untimely deaths avenged. Boone Helm, one of the most vile monsters of the West, finally met his end on January 14, 1864. The killing spree of the cut-throat cannibal was finally over.

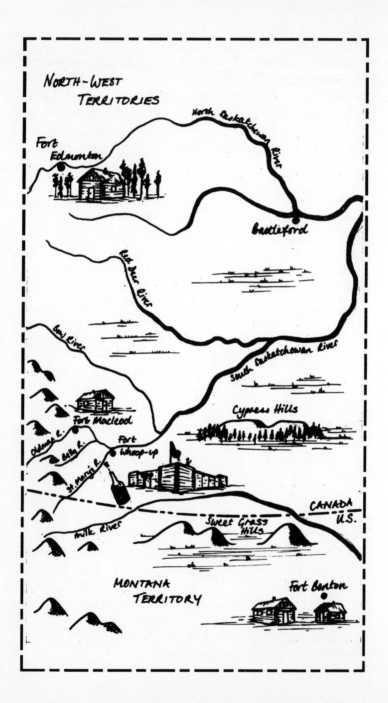

3

THE FORT WHOOP-UP BANDITS AND THE CYPRESS HILLS MASSACRE

...a new kind of bandit, intent on trading in illegal booze, packed up and headed north on what was dubbed the Whoop-Up trail.

One of the last great gang of thieves to rule the Canadian West was a rag-tag troop of American whiskey traders with names that sounded like they belonged on a carnival marquee. Waxy Weatherwax, Crazy Francois Vielle, Toe String Joe, Slippery Dick and Spring Heel Jack were some of the characters who occupied notorious Fort Whoop-Up in the latter half of the nineteenth century. Their chief claim to a dubious fame was their contribution to the devastation of local native populations by plying them with their stock trade of whiskey and guns.

The Whoop-Up bandits were eventually subdued by the long arm of the law. The red-coated North-West Mounted Police, the Dominion of Canada's newly created force set up to police the newly created North-West Territories, arrived in the nick of time, but not before a struggle ensued between the lawless American West and the new order imposed and sanctioned by the British Empire.

In 1869, two years after Confederation, the Hudson's Bay Company made a deal with Ottawa to sell Rupert's Land—large portions of what is now Quebec and Ontario, all of Manitoba, most of Saskatchewan, Alberta, Yukon and the Northwest Territories—to the Dominion of Canada. The prairies had been overrun with unemployed American soldiers following the end of the Civil War in 1865, and mercenaries, outlaws, soldiers of fortune, rootless drifters and hobos from the States migrated north where the land was held by whomever was willing to defend it.

The Canadian West was virtually unpoliced prior to the arrival of the Mounties in 1874, and many unscrupulous men decided a good living could be made trading rotgut whiskey to natives in exchange for bison skins that were in great demand in the more sophisticated and "civilized" American East.

Through the 1860s and 1870s dozens of independent traders headed north of the border beyond the range of the American Cavalry patrols to set up shop in guns, ammunition and alcohol.

First attempting to supply the ever-growing demand for drink from the backs of horse-drawn wagons, the whiskey traders soon learned that the wrath of an intoxicated or angry native was no laughing matter. They needed protection and the fewer face-to-face dealings with the natives the better. Fortified stockades were set up with posts armed with rifle ports and loopholes in the walls for blasting attackers.

Alcohol consumption soon became widespread and the Indians suffered miserably. The Peigan, Blood and Blackfoot quickly became addicted to the potent brew of raw alcohol which was often flavoured with molasses for taste, or tea for colour. It was not uncommon when a brave traded everything he owned for the white man's burning firewater.

The great herds of buffalo that roamed the prairies suffered greatly with the arrival of the whiskey traders. Buffalo were slaughtered by the thousands, and by the time the NWMP arrived from eastern Canada, the buffalo herds of the western prairies were virtually eliminated. The natives, whose way of life was closely tied to the buffalo, were a broken, demoralized, hungry and addicted people, sold off in the name of American profits to a bunch of bandits.

The most notorious fort of the dozen or so that sprang up in the land north of the Montana Territory was Fort Whoop-Up, near what is today Lethbridge, Alberta. In 1869 a couple of ruthless businessmen named Al Hamilton and John Healy selected a site at the junction of the Oldman and St. Mary rivers. The partners built a collection of log cabins surrounded by a flimsy wooden stockade, and began trade in a foul and intoxicating brew that they passed off as whiskey to unsuspecting natives.

In its first six months the whiskey trade yielded a return of some $50,000 in profits for Hamilton and Healy. The buffalo hides poured into the fort, and the rotgut flowed out. The exchange of goods meant major money for the men who sat inside the walls of the fort.

Word soon got out in the northwestern States and a new kind of bandit, intent on trading in illegal booze, packed up and headed north on what was dubbed the Whoop-Up trail between Fort Benton, a post in Montana Territory on the Missouri River, and the Dominion of Canada's own Fort Whoop-Up. It was a pathway to disaster.

FORT WHOOP-UP

Realizing the impact that firewater was having on their people, a group of angry natives turned on the whiskey traders in 1870 and burned the original fort to the ground. But their defiance wasn't enough to stop the lucrative operation of Fort Whoop-Up. Healy and Hamilton simply decided to rebuild the fort, and this time they made sure that it was "Indian proof."

The second fortress was impenetrable as well as huge. It took thirty men over two years to construct it, and by the time it was completed in 1874, Whoop-Up was a square-timber structure with thick walls, again loopholed for rifles. This time, however, the four bastions on the corners of the rectangular fort were fitted with weapons, one housing a small cannon and the other a howitzer. Gunmen carrying rifles and long "Indian disposal" poles patrolled the stockade. If a native was caught scaling the walls of the fort, he would be pushed back down. If he made a second attempt to gain access to the fort, he was shot.

Windows and doors in the new Fort Whoop-Up were fitted with iron bars, as were the chimney tops. The only contact between the traders inside and the natives outside were three wickets near the gates of the fort. Here the natives fed their buffalo hides and other pelts into a narrow grate. The furs were retrieved, appraised behind closed doors and a tin cup of rotgut—raw alcohol sometimes poisoned with tobacco juice for colour, or infused with laudanum, an opium substance, or Jamaican ginger or pepper for the throat-burning effect—would be handed out as payment.

Fort Whoop-Up didn't only trade illegal alcohol. It also set itself up as the post for war surplus blankets as well as rifles and ammunition. High-powered repeating rifles became second only to rotgut in their popularity. Although a surplus of these rifles existed on the market south of the line following the Civil War, they were still considered precious by Indians who had only just been introduced to the ancient single-shot muzzle-loading rifles a few decades earlier. Guns and alcohol made for a deadly combination with the plains Indians—a nomadic people, once self-sufficient, became very dependent on white man's wares.

Reverend John McDougall, a Methodist missionary who observed the plunder of Fort Whoop-Up in its heyday, reported chaos in Indian camps that were ruled by alcohol. Many people remained drunk for days on end. He reported drinking sprees too numerous to number in any given week, which often included an entire camp. Murder and stabbings within the native settlements were much more frequent since the introduction of alcohol and it was not uncommon for unattended children wandering the settlements to be mauled, killed and occasionally consumed by packs of hungry camp dogs.

With lawlessness abounding and no civil or legal institutions at hand, Ottawa began to worry that the U.S. Cavalry might simply ride across the international boundary and take charge. Politicians were right to be worried. The Canadian government's decision to take action against the American traders and their whiskey forts was spurred on by concerns about sovereignty more than by concerns for the indigenous people whose culture was taking such a brutal beating at the hands of the whiskey robbers.

The impetus for Ottawa's eventual response to the crisis in the West started with an incident in May 1873, when a group of wolfers calling themselves the Green River Renegades massacred a band of Assiniboine Indians in the Cypress Hills.

The Green River Renegades were a group of a dozen men, mostly American, and some Canadian, intent on seeking revenge on a party of Indians who had allegedly stolen their horses. The history of the wolfers and the Indians had never been good. The Green River Renegades were killing packs of wolves by baiting the animals with poisoned buffalo carcasses. What they failed to realize was the sacred nature of wolves in the native culture. Wolves were highly respected, and the natives felt a remarkable kinship with the animal. Whether the Indians were subconsciously able to draw a parallel between the poisoning of the wolves and their own depleted numbers being taken by alcohol is questionable but, regardless, a clash between wolfers and the natives usually meant a bloody confrontation.

It was in spring 1873, when the Green River Renegades from Fort Benton, 100 miles south of the Cypress Hills in what is now Saskatchewan, rode to Canada on a vigilante mission. Led by a man named John Evans, the posse was an angry group. Their horses had been stolen, and someone—although they weren't quite sure who—was going to pay.

The wolfers trailed the supposed thieves to within a few miles of the whiskey post, Fort Farwell, until the trail suddenly went cold. Evans, set on vengeance, decided that Fort Farwell was a perfect place to fortify his men's spirits. He decided to do that with whiskey and loud talk. All twelve horsemen rode into the fort and bellied up to the makeshift bar.

"Seen any Indians around?" Evans asked proprietor Abel Farwell.

"A camp of Assiniboines up river. Why?"

"Stole our horses," grunted Evans, throwing back his second straight whiskey.

"Wouldn't be the Assiniboines," cautioned Farwell, ever-mindful of the tension between wolfers and natives. "That band has been wintering way north of here. No way they could have stolen horses below the line. Besides," he added, fixing Evans with a steely gaze, "they ain't big on horses. I've only seen three or four ponies at Little Soldier's camp. I doubt very much you got the right Indians."

"Little Soldier?"

"The chief of the band. They're camped up river a piece," replied Farwell.

Evans only grunted and ordered another bottle of whiskey, which was soon demolished by his men. Farwell was right.

Trouble was brewing. It escalated when trader George Hammond walked into Farwell's. He worked at Mose Solomon's, a whiskey run across from Farwell's, and recently he'd had a horse stolen and was now claiming that some thieving Indian was asking for a reward for the pony's return.

"Probably the same fellow who stole her, wants the reward," he muttered to Evans, pulling up a glass and helping himself to the open bottle. "I paid him off with a bottle of whiskey but I swear he's the same one who nabbed my horse in the first place. All we got around here is a bunch of horse-thieving red-skins."

Those were the words the wolfers were waiting for. They drank the night away and didn't stop until the sun poked its head over the horizon. Unfortunately, the natives at Little Soldier's camp were also drinking whiskey. Two drunken camps of people and a natural animosity made a day ripe for violence, and it took only one small incident to ignite the short fuse of the drunken wolfers.

Again, it was George Hammond who fired things up. His horse, the one whose return he'd paid off with a bottle of hooch, was gone again. He wanted the thieving Indians to pay.

Hammond, Evans and the gang of eleven other wolfers agreed that it was time to let the Indians have it. They rode into Little Soldier's camp demanding to know where their horses were. If it weren't for tempers fueled by alcohol, the Cypress Hills Massacre might never have been. As it was, the natives taunted the men, and the wolfers responded by opening fire.

Of the thirteen wolfers, one was lost. An American named Ed Grace took an arrow in the chest. Of the Indians, thirty braves were butchered by the high-powered repeating rifles.

The Assiniboines didn't stand a chance. Women and children fled the lodges as their chief was murdered. The wolfers, enraged, cut off Little Soldier's head, mounted it on a long pole and paraded through the plundered camp as a warning to other Indians. After burying Grace, the wolfers returned to the gates of Farwell's fort, bearing the grisly remains of the chief. His severed head was a terrible reminder to natives and Indian sympathizers not to mess with the white wolfers.

The next morning, Evans and his lot were gone, headed back to Fort Benton boasting of cleansing the north of some hot-tempered, red-skinned horse thieves. The folks in the Montana Territory saw the Cypress Hills Massacre as a white man-over-red man conquest but not the Canadians. When word of the slaughter got back to Prime Minister John A. Macdonald, he visualized American bandits raiding the West with a view to subjugating all and any Canadian presence. The West wasn't safe from Americans. Alcohol was ruining the indigenous people. Macdonald decided to take no chances. He had to establish a police presence in the West. He stepped up the recruiting of men to form the North-West Mounted Rifles, a name that was changed a few months later to the North-West Mounted Police.

On July 8, 1874 a force of some 275 men, 310 horses, 142 oxen, 114 Red River carts, 93 head of cattle, 73 wagons, and a huge stash of extra ammunition and supplies set out from Fort Dufferin in Manitoba for the rumoured, and much maligned Fort Whoop-Up. The objective? Quash the whiskey traders and establish law and order in the untamed land.

Under Commissioner George French the march west proved much more difficult than anyone could possibly have imagined. Mosquitoes, heat, drought, dwindling food supplies, a lack of wood for fires, sickness, poor and ill-informed guides—all of these plagued the red-coated Mounties in their 800-mile trek.

On July 29, Inspector W.D. Jarvis and Sergeant Sam Steele split off from the main troop and led twenty men, fifty-five carts and the weakest of the livestock on the northern route to Fort Edmonton. The other group continued south following roughly the route taken by the men who surveyed the international boundary two years earlier. By early September the weather was turning.

French suspected the Metis guides he had hired were actually from Fort Whoop-Up and were leading his troop the wrong way. The truth of the matter was that the southern group of Mounties were lost on the prairies. Horses were dying. Men, forced to drink what water there was from stagnant swamps, were infected with raging dysentery and became close to dying as well. Almost 750 miles from Dufferin with winter descending, French and his troop were in trouble. At the confluence of the Bow and Belly rivers, the location of the rumoured Whoop-Up whiskey fort, French could only find three abandoned log huts.

Fearing for the safety of his men, he decided to spilt the column a third time, leaving 150 men under Assistant Commissioner James F. Macleod in the Sweet Grass Hills near the Montana Territory border. French took a smaller group of men and headed south to Fort Benton to buy supplies and hire a guide to lead them the rest of the way to Fort Whoop-Up.

French's luck was with him. For ninety dollars a month, short, bowlegged Metis scout Jerry Potts promised to take the North-West Mounted Police to their destination. Potts was an excellent guide who knew the countryside well. The child of a Scottish fur-trading father and a Blood Indian mother, Potts had spent his childhood between Indian camps and white settlements. He was equally comfortable in both worlds. Although a man of few words, he knew the lay of the land sufficiently that the NWMP were able to regroup on the Milk River and, led by the silent Potts, continue their march to Fort Whoop-Up.

On October 9, 1874, the famed Mounted Police force came to an abrupt halt. Cresting a bluff on the Oldman River, Assistant Commissioner James Macleod, accompanied by 150 policemen and two nine-pound field guns, rode within firing range of the barricaded whiskey fort. The American flag—the stars and stripes—flew over the fort despite it being well north of the boundary.

While the field guns were trained on the fort, Macleod and Potts walked up to the huge timber doors and knocked. To their surprise, the gates were immediately opened and the NWMP were invited inside. American trader David Akers explained that his partners were away on business and would the weary troops like to have some tender buffalo steaks? The hospitality was completely unexpected. While Macleod and his men were anticipating a bloody siege, the whiskey traders had dumped, or moved, their wares. Fort Whoop-Up was as clean as the bald prairie. Not a drop of illegal liquor was found on the premises.

Impressed with the fort's construction, and knowing his men needed permanent shelter, Macleod offered to buy the building for $10,000 with the notion of turning it into a police post. Akers refused, however, insisting the building was worth more than twice that amount. The two men couldn't come to an agreement.

The only thing they did agree upon—and it was an unspoken agreement—was that with red coats within the walls of Fort Whoop-Up the whiskey trade was well and truly over. Without firing a shot, without having to attack the heavily fortified Fort Whoop-Up, the North-West Mounted Police, by their trek across more than 800 miles of trackless prairie, by their perseverance, and by their mere presence, had stemmed the liquor traffic in the Canadian West. The untamed area had been secured. An era of lawlessness had, at last, come to an end.

Lake Winnipeg

Stony Mountain Penitentiary

Selkirk

Assiniboine River

Winnipeg

Portage La Prairie

Red River

St. Boniface

Rat Portage

Lake of the Woods

MANITOBA

Dufferin

Emerson

CANADA

U.S.

Pembina

DAKOTA TERRITORY

Red River

N

Fargo

4

MANITOBA MEDLEY

In these pre-automobile, pre-railway days the criminal element in the province was surprisingly active and mobile. No small number of outlaws teemed in the grasslands, crossing back and forth across the border as the need for escape varied.

The 1870s was an eventful decade for Manitoba. The decade started with a bang when Louis Riel and his provisional government took control of the area, the upshot of which was the creation of what was called "The Postage Stamp Province." Its roots went back to 1812 when a group of Scottish settlers came out to the Red River Colony under the auspices of the Earl of Selkirk. Caught between the North West Company and the Hudson's Bay Company, and struggling to plant roots on the bald prairie south of Lake Winnipeg at the confluence of the Red and Assiniboine rivers, the colony witnessed a massacre at Seven Oaks, floods, famine, epidemics and the political uprising under Riel. When the last was resolved in 1870 with the creation of the province, there seemed renewed hope in the viability of the settlement. In 1871, with the creation of

British Columbia far away to the west, a railway was promised which would help secure the future prosperity of the community.

In the 1870s the province was sparsely settled, with little communities scattered great distances from one another across the plains. When Winnipeg was incorporated as a city in 1873, it had a population of about 3700 and a cityscape dominated by shacks. There was no where else to go but up.

Richard Power was only nineteen years old when he joined the original group of nineteen men on the newly formed Manitoba Provincial Police in October 1870. By February 1874, the year the North-West Mounted Police marched west from Fort Dufferin, Manitoba, Power had become Chief Constable of the provincial force. Although his meteoric rise through the ranks had been accomplished partly through the resignation, drunkenness or insubordination of his colleagues, his years on the force saw great skill and planning in strategies to round up the evil forces in his community.

THE MAIN STREET OF WINNIPEG, C. 1873

In these pre-automobile, pre-railway days the criminal element in the province was surprisingly active and mobile. No small number of outlaws teemed in the grasslands, crossing back and forth across the border as the need for escape varied. South of the border in Dakota Territory, there seemed to be a larger scope of criminals intent on not being noticed. Pembina, just south of the line, had an officer, as did faraway Fargo, but there was little else in the way of lawmen in these border areas of the U.S. Chief Constable Power's realm did not include Winnipeg itself—the city had its own force under the charming Chief Jack Ingram—but he had men at various points in the province. He also packed a .45 Colt revolver with a huge nine-inch barrel—the largest of its type made—and plenty of ammunition strapped to his waist.

One of Chief Constable Power's first cases was in June 1874 when a soldier, Joseph Michaud, stabbed an innocent passerby, James Brown, over thirty times. Michaud and some pals had knocked back a few too many after going AWOL. They got into a brawl, Brown stepped in to offer assistance

and was killed on the spot. Brown's stature in the community was such that there was talk of a lynching, since there was no doubt as to the killer. But the next morning Power outsmarted the gathering crowd by picking Michaud up at the barracks, arresting him, and hiding him in a wagon for what he planned as a convoluted route to the log jail behind the Post Office in Winnipeg.

Michaud was quickly convicted of murder and sentenced to hang in late August 1874. The quick-thinking forces of justice soon realized with consternation that there was no qualified hangman in the community. After trying out several wannabes, Winnipeg's Chief Jack Ingram settled on a Hudson's Bay Company cook named Robert Hodson to do the job. Hodson dispatched Michaud according to his temporary job description of the day, and then while Michaud was cut from the rope and went on to his final reward Hodson presumably went back to slinging hash and eggs for the fur trading empire. He took the occasional break from bacon and beans, evidently, as he later became famous in a modest way as the hangman at Battleford after the 1885 North-West Rebellion.

Meanwhile, Power had moved on to his next major case. In an odd coincidence, Michaud actually shared a cell with Gilbert Godon, an outlaw of Metis origins whose boozing and subsequent brawling with soldiers at Fort Garry after the 1869–70 Rebellion gained him some notoriety. Power had stopped a bullet intended for saloonkeeper Dugald Sinclair of the Pride of the West Saloon during an ugly episode between soldiers and Metis that ran a little out of hand. Wounded slightly in the right arm, he was treated and released with no charges laid against the Metis or soldiers involved. As might be expected, Sinclair was eternally grateful.

A few years later, on the evening of October 10, 1873, Godon and some intoxicated supporters arrived in the community of Dufferin at the home of a Mr. Fawcett to partake in his illegal supply of liquor. It appears that they were rebuffed, and a melee erupted. Godon stepped in to defend Fawcett against some members of his own group of pals, including a Benjamin Marchand. Godon got a shovel to the head for his efforts, although in gratitude Fawcett found some liquor after all and was able to provide some further entertainment for the remaining members of Godon's supporters.

A short while later, Godon was threatened by young Marchand in the yard outside Fawcett's. Godon grabbed a handy axe and slammed it into Marchand's head. Someone tried to pull Godon away, but he struck young Marchand again. Fawcett realized that with Fort Garry nearly sixty-five miles away, his best bet for control of the situation was the Canadian Boundary Commission then headquartered near Dufferin. He hot-footed it there and returned with some fifteen men, but they would not take responsibility for holding Godon even though Marchand succumbed to his injuries shortly after their arrival. Released, Godon high-tailed it to Dakota Territory, where he remained until picked up after another fight in Pembina some six months later.

Chief Constable Richard Power himself took on the responsibility of bringing our boy home. Back at Winnipeg, June 19, 1874, Godon pleaded not guilty to the charge of murder. The jury found him guilty and sentenced him to fourteen years. He escaped the provincial penitentiary on September 25, 1876, (picked up his wife and a horse) and again high-tailed it to Dakota Territory. Until August 1877 he was on the lam, flitting from one side of the line to the other.

On August 18, Customs Agent F.T. Bradley attempted to collect Godon in Emerson, just north of Pembina on the Canadian side of the border. In the subsequent melee, involving not only Godon's mother but also his sister-in-law, Godon vanished out the door. Bradley's deputies were unsuccessful in capturing him, and off Godon went to Dakota Territory again.

He was picked up in late February 1878 in Pembina, again after boozing and brawling had erupted into a date with a cell in the local slammer. This time his cellmates were a wife-killer and an embezzler, and the trio plotted their escape while chatting and chopping wood in the prison yard. They hit the road in the middle of the night of June 25, 1880. The embezzler ended up a respectable member of the Winnipeg real estate community; Godon and the wife-killer seem to have breezed off westward, where the latter died of exposure and the former was never seen again.

Chief Constable Richard Power, in the mean time, bent his powerful attention on other elements of the criminal scene. One of these elements was Edward Couture and his gang, based south of Pembina, who raided horses from farms on the sunny side of the line before fleeing south into Dakota Territory. The ever-alert Customs Officer F.T. Bradley had noticed one of the gang, Edward Martin, heading north in early September 1874 and let Power know. Chief Constable Power and Constable Heusens rode into the area late on September 7, and soon after Martin and a colleague, Charles Garden, entered the scene on horseback. They were collected immediately and planned to settle for the night at the stagecoach station. It was not to be.

Martin vaulted himself at Power and while the Chief struggled to regain his balance, shot at him at point-blank range.

He missed, Power recovered and the two wrestled. Meanwhile, Garden, acting on a signal from Martin, plunged the room into darkness by swiping the lamp from the table. He pulled out his knife and began a mighty tussle with Constable Heusens. Heusens had considerable bulk and height in his favour; after driving Garden into a wall, he leaped to Power's assistance. Martin still had his revolver and fired off a couple of shots; Garden spooked and hit the road.

Power pulled his powerful mighty Colt on Martin and quelled the action immediately and, while Heusens stood guard, went off in search of Garden. Near the corral he fired a couple of shots into the darkness but soon realized the futility of the search. The next morning Heusens and Martin returned to Winnipeg while Power located Garden, who had in fact been wounded in the darkness, and headed home.

By October 1, Martin was gone again, having picked the locks with accomplice Charles Bigeral and escaped with the help of fellow gang members. They were captured in Minnesota on October 28 and thrown into jail in Moorhead, Dakota Territory. His cell had double locks and as well he had to submit to wearing leg irons. These acted as no deterrent to the irrepressible lock picker. On the lam again on May 5, 1875, he continued his horse-thieving ways farther west. He was captured, sentenced to a fairly hefty term, which he served fully before fading into the dusty trails of history. The rest of the Couture gang was gradually rounded up.

Edward Daniels' involvement with Chief Constable Power began in mid-June 1875 when he began a sentence for theft. He and a group of fellow inmates escaped in mid-September and he began a life in Deadwood, Dakota Territory, where gunfights were commonplace. He returned to Winnipeg in 1876 and was apprehended on a stolen horse on October 25.

In June 1877 he was sentenced to two years, which he served before returning to crime in 1879. His intelligent career seemed to involve returning to Winnipeg and stealing the same things from the same group of people, sometimes using the disguise of a woman in a poor effort to conceal his identity. During this time he dropped his diary, thus informing police of his activities during the previous few years.

Finally, Power resorted to misleading Daniels into thinking he was searching another part of the province for the criminal. The strategy worked, and Daniels' location was pinpointed to a bedroom in St. Paul's. As Power slipped into the room, Daniels pulled the trigger of his revolver, but it misfired. He grabbed for a second revolver, but it was too late. As he looked down the barrel of Power's mighty revolver, he must have realized that defeat was the better part of valour. He was eventually sentenced to fourteen years, but he escaped the gallows on account of his gun misfiring at that critical moment.

Chief Constable Power's final case turned out to be the result of another escape from prison; this time, a talkative pickpocket named Mike Carroll drifted in from the East, evidently having created somewhat of a career out of jailbreaking. Unable to repress pride in his activities, he soon attracted the attention of the police in Winnipeg and they contrived to pick him up in a hotel dining room. Carroll seems to have been fleet of foot, more so than the unfortunate detective charged with apprehending him. But once again, his loose tongue created trouble for him and he ended up back in the slammer. A scant two weeks later, on July 23, he escaped on foot, sans shoes, and was seen beetling towards the Red River.

Constable Bell notified Chief Constable Power, who felt obligated to leave his sickbed to help capture the career escape artist and robber. They tracked Carroll down to a haystack near St. Norbert. Carroll, feet bruised and bleeding, surrendered gracefully when faced with the enormous Colt .45, and together the three propelled a commandeered railway handcar back to St. Boniface, across the river from Winnipeg.

By this time the ferry driver had retired for the evening, so it was decided to accept the offer of a fellow with a rowboat to complete their journey. But it was a fateful decision. Power evidently climbed into the boat first, handcuffed to Carroll. Somehow, whether by accident or design, the two went overboard and were never seen alive again. Power's powerful sidearm weighed heavily against him, as did his ammunition belt, for he didn't stand a chance against the powerful current and sank like a stone into the murky maelstrom. The pickpocket and jailbird's body washed ashore downstream.

Chief Constable Power, whose career with the Manitoba Police Force began at age nineteen, gave ten of the best years of his life to capturing jailbirds, murderers and robbers; the community responded with a full military funeral and accolades by the hundreds. His sudden and unexpected death by drowning left that community bereft and grieving.

SWIFT RUNNER

5

THE CANNIBAL SWIFT RUNNER FEARS WINDIGO

The spirit of Windigo could be Swift Runner's only justification for a terrible, terrible crime that shocked white settlers and native tribesmen alike.

Standing on the gallows on the bitterly cold morning of December 20, 1879, Kakusikutchin (or Katistchen; the spelling varies in written Cree), whose name translates to Swift Runner, looked across the prairies towards Fort Edmonton for the final time. It is impossible to know what the man with the blank face was thinking, but doubtless his mind was divided.

He was being hanged in Fort Saskatchewan for murder. More horrifying yet, the charges involved acts of cannibalism. The previous winter he had slaughtered and consumed his wife, his six children, his brother and his mother. Of that there was no doubt. But the tales of Windigo, the evil spirit that takes possession of a person's mind, spirit and body, which were once told to him by his grandfather, may have flashed into Swift Runner's mind.

In native mythology, Windigo possesses a person, turns their heart to ice and causes them to hunger after human flesh. A Windigo spirit in human form can be quelled only in fiery death. Natives believe the body must be burned, the ice heart melted, in order to stop Windigo's repellent desire to eat its own kind. Tragically, however, Swift Runner was dying the white man's way. The scaffold and noose about his neck were not a traditional cure for Windigo.

The spirit of Windigo could be Swift Runner's only justification for a terrible, terrible crime that shocked white settlers and native tribesmen alike, and instigated the first hanging by the North-West Mounted Police.

Mere hours earlier, Swift Runner, the self-proclaimed cannibal, had participated in a ritual that some could call spiritual or symbolic cannibalism. He had taken the sacrament of the Eucharist, a Christian service where communicants partake either literally or figuratively in the blood and body of Jesus Christ. For Swift Runner, conversion was an act of contrition. He had at last confessed his crime and believed he had been forgiven. On the day of his death, it is likely he recalled the teachings of his youth, when the Cree notion of God was the Great Spirit and the hideous act that had brought him to be hanged could only be caused by the devil Windigo.

Swift Runner's life is a complex study in duality. His story is a tale of two cultures and a man caught between two ways of life.

While records are somewhat incomplete, it appears Swift Runner was born around 1839 in a Cree camp in what is now central Alberta. Buffalo were plentiful on the prairies and no cattle grazed west of Lake Superior. It was thirty-five years before the North-West Mounted Police made their famous march west.

In a small band of wandering Cree, Swift Runner became a good hunter and a skilled leader. His life was typical of a young native man in the mid-1800s. It consisted of initiation rites, bear and buffalo hunting, pipe offerings to the Great Spirit and battles with the neighbouring Blackfoot nation to the south. A fine rider and the owner of a prized pony, Swift Runner was built like a warrior. He was described by journalists and traders as a tall, strong man with a narrow waist and large, muscled shoulders. He stood approximately six feet three inches tall and weighed just over 200 pounds.

Between 1855 and 1872 Swift Runner married and fathered six children, three boys and three girls, some of whom according to records of the time, were baptized by the district priest as a precautionary measure against death by epidemic. The prairies were prone to outbreaks of disease. Smallpox spread across the plains like wildfire, leaving native families, who had no immunity to the white man's illness, particularly devastated.

While exact numbers were never recorded, historians estimate that almost fifty percent of Alberta's native and Metis populations were wiped out by disease in the 1800s. Swift Runner's young family was not touched by the epidemic but a growing sense of despair permeated the native culture by the time he had established a family and was raising his own offspring.

In 1872 the Canadian government passed the *Dominion Lands Act* to prepare for the full-fledged influx of the white settlers to western Canada. In 1874, Prime Minister John A. Macdonald, fearing the Canadian West would become like the lawless, bandit-ridden west of the United States, sent the red-coated North-West Mounted Police to the North-West Territories to guard Canadian land, people and property. Approximately 300 men, holding the full weight of the authority of the Canadian government, rode from Manitoba to patrol and enforce law in a region larger than western Europe.

The North-West Mounted Police brought Queen Victoria's authority to Swift Runner's people, but with them also came disease, starvation, guns and the strange liquid that burned when lit—firewater.

Swift Runner had provided traditionally for his family, hunting and living off the land. In 1875, however, as he reached his mid-thirties, he was hired by the Hudson's Bay Company who later recommended him as a guide to the North-West Mounted Police.

Association with the Mounties and the white man's settlement brought the temptation of alcohol, and Swift Runner soon found himself returning to his family empty-handed. He had nothing to show for his work but pounding headaches and vague memories of strong drink.

On December 24, 1878, Swift Runner was arrested in Fort Saskatchewan for threatening and attempting to kill a white trader after a drunken quarrel. The Hudson's Bay Company wanted nothing more to do with him. He was jailed overnight and told to leave the settlement.

In today's society, Swift Runner would be considered a man suffering from mental illness. He began reporting to Reverend Father Hippolyte Leduc, an Oblate priest who ministered to him in his last days, that he "heard voices inside his head," and felt detached from the world. Coupled with the great change of life brought to the native population with the coming of white authority, Swift Runner became deeply depressed.

The winter of 1878–79 was particularly difficult for native people living in the St. Albert and Lac Ste. Anne area (northeast of Fort Edmonton) where Swift Runner had moved his family in an attempt to get back in touch with his own traditions. The once-plentiful buffalo were in short supply that winter.

A century earlier in 1754, Anthony Henday, the first white man credited with exploring central and northern Alberta, recorded buffalo numbering in the hundreds of thousands. By the time Swift Runner was a child, massive organized hunts of bison were underway. Between 1860 and 1875—largely as a way to control the native people—settlers slaughtered millions of buffalo, with much meat going to waste. There were reports of a buffalo hunt near St. Laurent in 1872 which recorded 600 buffalo killed in one day. In 1878, only five years later, the herds were diminished enough that Americans united to burn a strip of prairie south of the Canadian border in an attempt to keep herds from migrating north.

In July of that year not one herd of buffalo was sighted between Battleford and the Cypress Hills. Newly appointed Indian Commissioner Edgar Dewdney visited Fort Saskatchewan in 1879 and reported 1300 Indians so weak from hunger they could barely move.

Swift Runner's family, camped sixty-five miles northeast of Fort Saskatchewan in the Sturgeon River area, were in poor physical shape by the onset of winter. The weather was growing colder. There was very little food. His family was hungry and the pressure on Swift Runner was mounting. He feared the evil spirit of Windigo was upon him.

According to the confession told to Father Leduc following the horrific murders, Swift Runner and some of his extended family first killed and ate their dogs in an effort to keep themselves alive. By mid-February 1879, the dogs long since dead and eaten, Swift Runner realized there was nothing left to hunt. Swift Runner had heard rumours that the Canadian government was distributing 1400 pounds of beef to starving natives, so he persuaded his mother and brother to leave for Egg Lake where other Cree were camped. With a mounting sense of doom, Swift Runner's wife and all but one small son left camp, hoping their trek through the deep snow would result in food for their empty bellies. What happened next defies reason.

The ten-year-old boy who stayed behind was sleeping when Swift Runner's hallucinations started. Driven by madness, he began to visualize the child not as human but as a breathing, living animal—food for his immense and long-suppressed appetite. All moral codes, all sense of love and caring left him as he broke the ultimate taboo. According to Swift Runner, he was in the possession of Windigo when he put a gun to his son's skull. According to the account taken by the confessional priest, when the child did not die immediately, Swift Runner stabbed him repeatedly all the while weeping, before finally finishing him off with blows from a stick.

Using a sharp axe to remove the flesh from his son's body, Swift Runner roasted the meat and consumed it. He sucked the marrow from the tiny bones and ate the corpse between periods of feasting and deep, almost unconscious torpor. He lived on the meat for a few days before hunger, and madness, again overtook him.

The cannibal tracked down his wife and five other children, telling them the child at camp had died of starvation. Whether or not his family believed him will never be known, but weakened by hunger and bound by the chill of winter, they had little choice but to follow him back to the scene of the murder.

That night, claiming he had been "pushed by an evil spirit," Swift Runner massacred the rest of his family. He first shot his wife, killing her with a bullet to the neck. The sound of the shot and perhaps her groans of agony must have roused the children. Hastily, Swift Runner completed his murderous work.

His seven-year-old son was spared the hatchet that first stunned, then ended the lives of his three little sisters and his older brother. The remaining son was ordered to gather snow for melting, while his father cut the five bodies into pieces small enough for the cooking pot.

In Father Leduc's translation of Swift Runner's confession, the cannibal recalled breaking the skulls of his victims and taking out the brains. Any flesh that wasn't cooked hung on trees around the camp while the two remaining family members, father and son, sat at the fire and fed on their loved ones. The death camp became littered with skulls and bones, many of which, the police later discovered, were sucked clean of their marrow.

What propelled Swift Runner back into the woods after killing and consuming his wife, a son and three daughters is a mystery, but if the legend of Windigo is to be believed, it confirms the notion that this evil spirit, once tasting human flesh, cannot be satisfied without more of the same.

Swift Runner admitted to police he had travelled through the bush until he found the camp of his brother and mother. He killed them both, carrying their bodies back to camp for consumption. He told the Mounties who guarded him after his arrest that his mother was not tender like the children but "tough" and more difficult to chew.

Only the youngest boy remained, a witness to the terrible, unspeakable crime of murder and cannibalism. Swift Runner assured him he would be safe.

It was at last spring 1879, and the sloughs were melting and attracting wild birds. The woods were coming to life and starvation was no longer an issue for Swift Runner and his child, but guilt was. Approaching Egg Lake, almost five miles northwest of today's Morinville, Swift Runner knew he would soon have to confront people. Questions would be asked about his family. Could the child keep silent?

Afraid of discovery, the cannibal committed his final crime. He later confessed to Father Leduc that "the devil took possession of my soul and I saw my son as a fat beaver." Swift Runner took his gun and put a bullet into his last remaining child. Like his siblings, the last witness to the cannibal's action was cooked and eaten. At last, in late March 1879, Swift Runner returned alone to the Roman Catholic Mission at the settlement of St. Albert.

His story to the priests was one of starvation and despair. He claimed his entire family had died during the terrible winter and he had survived only by living on the broth of a boiled tipi, chewing on rawhide and capturing the occasional squirrel.

The story rang false. Swift Runner did not look starving. His appearance was that of a sleek, well-fed man. Although the priests allowed him to stay at the Mission and prayed for his lost family, their suspicions grew. When questions about his family were continually evaded, and when he confessed the evil spirit of Windigo had been tormenting him in dreams, their fears grew.

There is no doubt Swift Runner was a favourite among the Mission schoolchildren. When not plagued by dreams or stupefied by guilt, he was known for his ability to tell stories and entertain with tales of the olden days. It was when the dark native with complex emotions tried to convince the Mission fathers he was the perfect candidate to lead the children on a traditional hunting trip that something twigged. The request troubled the Oblate priest on duty and he took his nagging suspicions about Swift Runner to the North-West Mounted Police. An arrest was not far off.

Inspector William Jarvis was an old war-hound seasoned in earlier African conflicts. After leading the "A" Division of the NWMP on the 1874 march west on the hostile northern route, he had taken up his post in the Fort Saskatchewan barracks as Area Superintendent. Like Father Leduc, Jarvis felt Swift Runner's motives were suspect. He had also heard rumours of the man's instability and moodiness. On May 27, 1879, Swift Runner was arrested and brought to Fort Saskatchewan for questioning.

Even though Swift Runner refused to change his story, Jarvis doubted his account of how starvation had killed his entire family. A search party, led by Sub-Inspector Severe Gagnon and Sergeant Richard Steele, was immediately dispatched to the Sturgeon River camp to gather evidence. On June 4, 1879 Swift Runner, shackled inside a Red River cart, accompanied the band of police to the death camp.

Realizing the evidence was against him, Swift Runner tried to escape on two occasions but both times was recaptured. His reluctance to participate proved to the Mounties something was badly amiss. When it became apparent he was leading them in circles, the authorities drugged him with a potent mix of plug tobacco dissolved in alcohol, hoping the swill would loosen his tongue. It worked. The next morning Swift Runner led the police to his camp, claiming on arrival

THE BONES OF SWIFT RUNNER'S VICTIMS

that animals would have by now taken away what was left of his wretched, starved family.

Eight human skulls were found in Swift Runner's camp. Bones picked clean by birds and rodents littered the camp. Evidence of death was all around. It was the discovery of the cooking pot, coated with human fat, and the small skull of Swift Runner's infant daughter, her eye sockets stuffed with a pair of stockings, that brought the terrible truth to light. Not only was he a multiple murderer, he was also a cannibal. Insanity, possession, mental illness aside, the police realized in horror the man had killed and eaten his entire family.

Back in Fort Saskatchewan, justice was rapid. Swift Runner's trial took place August 16, 1879, with Stipendiary Magistrate Richardson presiding. The evidence was damning. The prisoner had offered a brief, incomplete confession. It took the six-man jury less than half an hour to announce a guilty verdict. Swift Runner was to die in the gallows December 20 at 10 a.m. The sentence was confirmed by Ottawa, and the Minister of Justice forwarded the death warrant to Inspector Jarvis. The Mounties of the West would hang their first man.

Swift Runner was still haunted by Windigo, and guards at the Fort Saskatchewan prison reported his behaviour as erratic and unpredictable. He would groan and screech and shake his manacled leg irons one moment, and be totally passive the next. It wasn't until November 30, twenty days before his execution, that Swift Runner was able to shake off what he believed to be the evil spirit of his forefathers.

Approached by Inspector Jarvis, Father Leduc agreed to minister to Swift Runner in his final weeks. As his death day approached, Swift Runner confessed the entire saga to Father Leduc, including the fact that he believed his terrible crime was committed by the powerful spirit of Windigo acting through him. Father Leduc was given permission to record, translate and publish Swift Runner's confession.

In his June 1880 report from the Mission to his superiors in France, Father Leduc claimed "the pagan, sadist, infidel and cannibal [had undergone] the influence of Holy Religion and a complete transformation."

Swift Runner seemed to welcome death following his religious conversion, but the question of hanging still presented problems. Indians in the area, despite having closed rank against the cannibal, were suspect of his method of death and even Swift Runner knew his body should be burned. However, it was the white man's law that prevailed.

Sheriff Edouard Richard of Battleford, then capital of the North-West Territories, set out by sleigh December 9 in minus fifty-six degree Fahrenheit to preside over the hanging. He arrived in Fort Saskatchewan, to the relief of Inspector Jarvis, the day before Swift Runner's execution.

Swift Runner and Father Leduc stood together on the scaffold on the morning of December 20. While Father Leduc prayed, a volunteer hangman placed the noose around Swift Runner's neck. A party of fifty spectators, mostly Metis and Indians, began drumming and singing furiously. They stopped only when the giant cannibal spoke his last words.

In Cree, Swift Runner thanked the Fathers for their mercy and the police for their kindness, and acknowledged that he had done wrong. He said he regretted his crime and asked people to pardon him. While government interpreter Gordon Brazeau translated, the trapdoor swung open, and the neck of the great cannibal Swift Runner snapped. He died instantly. The West had hanged its first, and no doubt, one of its most gruesome killers. The spirit of Windigo and the nine victims of Swift Runner all dangled at the end of a ten-foot length of rope.

Nicola Valley, B.C.

6

THE BROTHERS MCLEAN AND THEIR COHORT HARE: A GANG OF VIOLENT YOUTH

Allan, Charlie and Archie were reared on stories of Indian-killing exploits perpetrated by their renegade father, regardless of the fact that their mother was a full-blood member of the Kamloops tribe.

On the British Columbia coast, in the chilling winter way back in 1881, four wayward youths were hanged by the neck until dead. Hanged. Way off in the interior of the province, in Kamloops, where two terrible murders had occurred, the townsfolk rejoiced.

Archie McLean was just fifteen when he walked the scaffold steps up to the specially built, four-trapdoor gallows at the New Westminster Provincial Jail. He wasn't alone. Archie was accompanied by his two older brothers, seventeen-year-old Charlie and twenty-five-year-old Allan, and their wild-eyed friend Alexander Hare, also seventeen. Archie was among the youngest people ever executed in Canada. But despite his youth, this boy was bad clear through.

The McLean brothers and their sidekick Alex Hare cut a heartless swath of terror through the ranching country of the Nicola Valley and the southwestern Okanagan in the early winter of 1879. They murdered two men, one a Provincial Police constable killed in the heat of a gun battle, and the other an unsuspecting shepherd shot while tending his sheep. They terrorized countless ranching families and tried to incite a native uprising to rival the bloody rebellion of the fierce Chilcotin tribe that occurred in that same area near twenty years' previous.

As they died together, so the McLean brothers lived together in heartbreaking poverty and despair. The boys were ruled by the iron fist of their Scottish-born father Donald McLean, a man with deep racial prejudices that sprang to the surface in massive fits of murderous temper. An employee at the Hudson's Bay Company, Donald McLean was unpleasant and quarrelsome, disliked even by his own colleagues and compatriots.

Despite being twice married to native women, who collectively bore him eleven children, the elder McLean held a deep-seated grudge against native people. The sons of his second marriage, Allan, Charlie and Archie, were reared on stories of Indian-killing exploits perpetrated by their renegade father, regardless of the fact that their mother was a full-blood member of the Kamloops tribe.

In 1849 Donald McLean had led a sixteen-man posse in a revenge hunt. They were pursuing a Chilcotin brave, Tlel (also spelled Tlhelh is some accounts), who was suspected of killing Hudson's Bay Company employee, Alexis Belanger. With Tlel's cabin surrounded, McLean burst through the door, killing an unarmed man who claimed to be Tlel's uncle, and his stepdaughter and her nursing infant daughter.

The natives eventually got their revenge when they shot Donald McLean in the back as he participated in one of his favourite sports—Indian hunting—during the Chilcotin rebellion of the 1860s. On his death, it was discovered he wore a steel breast plate beneath his shirt, which perhaps explained how he managed to live as long as he did.

Allan was just a young lad when his father was killed and the two younger boys but babes, yet their father's legacy of hatred and murder was passed down to them. Not only did

ARCHIE MCLEAN   ALLAN MCLEAN

the boys seem predestined to the outlaw life, they were also genetically predisposed to inherit their father's Scottish looks: pale skin, dark hair and Caucasian features. While the younger McLeans were actually Metis, the native community didn't accept the boys as such; to the natives, the McLean boys were considered white. But to the white community, the native blood of the boys' mother determined that the McLean brothers were Indians. Thus ostracized from both groups in the community, they became isolated from the normal friendships of childhood.

Without the wages of a father, the McLean children grew up doing what they could to make a living. On the cattle and sheep ranches that had sprung up on the rich, short-grass grazing land between Ashcroft and Spences Bridge in the West and Kamloops and Douglas Lake in the East, the boys lived, for the most part, by their wits. They became known locally for their expert saddlemanship, their impeccable shooting skills, their ability to hunt and their seemingly unlimited capacity for drink. The three brothers learned early that the world owed them nothing. What they wanted they had to take, and take they did.

Horses, cattle, property, food, whiskey—the McLean boys knew no limits to their thievery. Any resistance was met with raw, dispassionate brutality. One account tells of a Chinese man robbed and beaten so severely by the McLeans that he almost died of his injuries.

Law officers in the Crown Colony of British Columbia had been present from the time it was established in 1858, shortly after gold was discovered on the Fraser River. Chief Inspector of Police, Chartres Brew, along with a handful of men, patrolled the vast wilderness by canoe and horseback in summer and by snowshoe and dog team in winter.

Small detachments were established at key geographical points in the colony as a means of controlling the rush of 30,000 gold-hungry men, most of them from the lawless American states, and most armed to the hilt. The police knew their task and executed it well, for despite the massive influx of people on the Coast and Interior of B.C., relatively few crimes were reported. In 1871 British Columbia joined Confederation on the lure of a railway to be built west across the formidable mountain barrier.

Provincial Police officer, Constable John Ussher, thirty-five, knew of the McLean brothers and their wild ways from the time he took on his posting in Kamloops. He'd had run-ins with all of the brothers at least once, charging them on minor offences. The McLeans were an uncontrollable bunch and over the years Ussher thought they were mean and getting meaner. Townsfolk were afraid to confront them and the constable felt mounting pressure to demonstrate to the boys the strong arm of the law.

His opportunity came the summer of 1877 when he arrested the middle brother, Charlie McLean, for assault. He was to serve a three-month sentence for biting off the tip of a man's nose in a bar room brawl. A Kamloops prison cell didn't sit pretty with the middle McLean. Serving less than a quarter of his sentence, Charlie broke out and linked up with his three brothers and their pal Alex Hare. The boys formed a marauding gang that, over the next few months, wreaked havoc all the way to the American border.

The incident that triggered death in the Nicola Valley began with a horse theft. Charlie McLean, a year and a half out of jail, had taken fancy to a large black stallion, the prized possession of a rancher named William Palmer. Palmer, who ran cattle on a spread thirty-five miles southwest of Kamloops, noticed the mount missing the same day he saw McLean blatantly riding the stolen horse near the foot of Long Lake.

He decided he'd get his animal back. Approaching the McLean camp cautiously, Palmer soon became aware that the boys had been drinking. Alex Hare was asleep on the ground, a bottle by his side. Archie was nowhere to be seen, but the two older brothers were at the camp, bristling at his approach. They were armed with two Colt .45 revolvers and at least three rifles. In a quick glance around the camp Palmer saw his horse tethered to a nearby tree.

"Looking for something?" snarled Allan, as Palmer reined in his mount.

"Just some company," responded Palmer.

"Look somewheres else," said Charlie, cocking his revolver and brandishing it, a strong indicator that Palmer should move on.

Wisely, the rancher retreated. He later told Constable Ussher he could hear the McLean brothers mocking him as he left the camp.

Ussher knew action had to be taken. The youth were running amok, paying no attention to authority, terrorizing good people with threats—and more and more often—with acts of violence. Telegraph messages to Victoria requesting more money to secure the jail after Charlie McLean's break had fallen on deaf ears or had not gotten through at all. In 1879 the Canadian Pacific Railway was still a long way from reaching Kamloops, and Ussher and other Provincial Police of his ilk were quite alone in their isolated detachments.

Ussher knew justice must be served, however. On December 7, 1879 he wrote a warrant for the arrest of the McLean gang.

As a precautionary measure, the constable hauled Hector McLean, the boys' older stepbrother, into the detachment for questioning and placed him under arrest. He swore in Palmer as a special constable, picked up well-respected tracker Amni Shumway and rancher John McLeod, then the foursome rode toward Long Lake.

The McLean camp appeared deserted when the small posse approached just after sunset that day in early December. The campfire still burned but the young men were nowhere in sight. From the suspicious silence a shot rang out, and a second later Palmer felt a bullet whiz through his beard and heard McLeod cry out in agony. He had been shot in the face, the bullet from Allan McLean's rifle shattering his cheek.

"Throw down your guns," called Ussher, slipping from the saddle and ducking behind his horse.

His answer was a barrage of bullets. One struck the wounded McLeod in the leg. Ussher, totally unarmed, proceeded towards the boys. He must have thought he could talk them into surrender, but in this instance he was sadly mistaken. Alex Hare jumped out from behind a thicket armed with a rifle and a large hunting knife. Ussher rushed toward Hare before he could get a shot away, but the young man, struggling, raised his knife and plunged it into the constable's chest. Again and again, Hare stabbed Ussher until the bleeding man fell to the ground. A split second later Archie McLean stepped forward and, from point-blank range, fired a merciful shot into Ussher's head. The lawman was dead, his fellow enforcers in hasty retreat.

The townspeople of Kamloops were incensed at the horrific murder of their young constable. Married not eighteen months, John Ussher was a popular presence in the frontier town. Immediately upon hearing of his death at the hands of the McLean gang, a larger posse was formed.

John Clapperton, Justice of the Peace in Kamloops, was immediately thrust to the foreground of the bloody drama. With Ussher's death, he was now the sole legal representative. He hastily telegraphed Victoria to get instruction from Provincial Police headquarters. Police Superintendent Charles Todd wired Constable James Lindsay at the Barkerville detachment northeast of Quesnel, telling him to meet another constable at Cache Creek, then hightail it to Kamloops. Headquarters also notified Washington Territory officials, telling them to mind the border crossings, particularly the one at Colville in the Okanagan Valley, in case the McLeans headed south across country to the United States.

Meanwhile, a group of angry and heavily armed men led by Clapperton and Kamloops merchant John Mara (an aspiring politician who was rumoured to have taken Annie McLean, the boys' sister, as his mistress) thundered back to the McLean camp only to find it abandoned with the terrible exception of Ussher's body, stripped of its coat, gloves and boots, lying frozen in blood-stained snow.

It stands to reason the McLean boys and their cohort Hare realized the gravity of their crime. Before December 7, they had been involved in thieving and fighting. Now they had murdered a member of the Provincial Police force. Deciding there was no turning back, they headed down the Nicola Valley and veered southeast towards Douglas Lake, with the posse close on their heels.

Their next victim was a man named James Kelly. Accounts differ as to his relationship with the McLean brothers. Some say Kelly was unknown to them, a drifter-cum-shepherd working for wages minding sheep, who was simply in the wrong place at the wrong time. Others claim he'd recently had one of the McLeans arrested for stealing a bottle of brandy. Either way, Kelly was used for target practice by the blood-fueled boys. The posse discovered Kelly's bullet-riddled body amid his sheep, the snow again stained with innocent blood. A watch and chain bearing Kelly's initials would later be found in the possession of Alex Hare.

At this point no one in the posse knew that young Charlie McLean had been wounded in the initial scrimmage. He was bleeding badly and needed his wounds tended to. The brothers stopped in at Tomas Trapp's ranch to allow Charlie to rest. They terrorized Trapp, an older man, and forced him to hand over all his guns and ammunition. According to Trapp, they gambled with his life, flipping a coin to see whether he would live or die.

Trapp was lucky that day. The bandits rode off with his liquor and his firearms, but after taunting him with the bloodied articles from Ussher's body, they let lady luck make the final call. Tails came up when the coin came down and Trapp was spared the fate of the luckless Kelly.

Next the outlaws rode to John Roberts' ranch, west of Douglas Lake. They boasted to Roberts of their exploits, and as if to make real their murderous intent, they held up grim souvenirs from the body of the slain constable. Ussher's canteen, his coat and the handcuffs he'd carried for the express purpose of arresting the McLean brothers, were each dangled before the horrified Roberts.

"I thought they were going to kill me, too," Roberts reported later, "but instead they asked the whereabouts of others. I guess they wanted to settle some scores on account of being hunted like they were. They were like [a pack of] mad dogs, wild and crazy, laughing out of control while they showed off what they'd done."

77

Onward they rode, stopping at ranches and homesteads, terrorizing and intimidating the innocent inhabitants with their tales of death and plunder. At each house they gathered liquor, guns and ammunition. It seemed Allan McLean had a plan. Likely remembering his father's tales of the Chilcotin uprising, he thought he'd turn tables on the pursuing posse. His idea was to arm the natives in order to precipitate another rebellion. This time, however, the McLeans would be on the side of the Indians. The white intruders, whose laws were forcing native people into poverty, would pay at last.

At the headwaters of the Nicola River, Allan McLean told Nicola tribe Chief Chillitnetza (some accounts spell his name Shillitnetza) of his scheme, hoping the chief would call a council of war and lend support to the outlaws. Chief Chillitnetza refused, advising the McLeans to make for the States rather than causing trouble in peaceful Nicola country.

The boys were now running scared. They carried on in a westerly course, stopping on December 10 at an abandoned cabin on Douglas Lake to see to Charlie's wounds and to formulate another plan. Word as to their whereabouts spread quickly, and the shack was already surrounded by local ranchers and cowboys by the time Clapperton and his posse caught up with the killer McLeans.

It was a pitiful siege. The lawmen knew Hare and the McLean brothers would eventually have to surrender. Time was certainly on the side of the posse. While Clapperton and his men made campfires and roasted food in the woods near the desperadoes' shack, the young outlaws poked sticks through the chinks in their fortress, trying to draw snow inside to quench their thirst.

Time and time again Clapperton called on the youths to sur-render, but his requests were met by occasional bursts of gunfire. All present at the site knew it was just a matter of time before the McLeans gave up the fight. Despite being heavily armed, the boys lacked food, water and warmth. A northerly December wind was blowing and the temperature was dropping steadily.

The posse, having divided into three shifts, was getting tired with the stand-off. On Friday, December 13, Clapperton decided to smoke the fugitives out of their hole. He ordered bales of hay to be soaked in kerosene, loaded onto the rot-ting frame of an old wagon, lit and pushed next to the wooden shack. The damp hay refused to light and the smouldering fire bomb had little effect but to madden the captive youths like wasps in their nest.

In a hail of gunfire the McLeans drove Clapperton's posse and their smoking wagon back to the edge of the woods, dropping one of his men in the process. The wounded man, who took a bullet to the chest, and the ineffectual smoking wagon, spelled victory for the outlaws and gales of laughter pursued the retreating men.

Victory was short lived, however. The next afternoon, December 14, 1879, Allan McLean admitted defeat for him-self and his trio of colleagues. Four filthy, thirsty, grim-faced youths emerged from the cabin carrying a small white flag. Before the eyes of the assembled masses, they pointed their rifles heavenward and fired off their remaining ammunition. It was a native tradition to fight until the last cartridge was fired, and Alex Hare and the brothers McLean, in a final act of rebellion, claimed their native ancestry before surrendering.

NEW WESTMINSTER PROVINCIAL JAIL

The preliminary hearing in Kamloops established the murder charges. Hare made a partial confession of guilt before the youths were shackled to their ponies to be transported overland to the province's nearest seat of justice in New Westminster. The journey took just under a week, in terrible conditions. The gang and their three guards traversed the Fraser River valley in a blinding blizzard and sub-zero temperatures. The murderers were finally locked up in the New Westminster Provincial Jail on Christmas Day, 1879.

The trial, in March 1880, was a rapid affair despite a plea for mercy on the part of the defence attorney who claimed the youths, given their violent upbringing, had not a chance to be worthy citizens. Their youth notwithstanding, Alex Hare and Allan, Charlie and Archie McLean were condemned to hang for the murders of James Kelly and Johnny Ussher. A useless appeal followed and on January 31, 1881, at 8:00 a.m. four trapdoors were simultaneously sprung. The wild McLean gang, defiant to the end, made Canadian history by their youth and their unshakable bond of brotherhood.

KICKING HORSE CANYON, B.C.

7

BULLDOG KELLY: TWO COUNTRIES AT ODDS OVER THE FATE OF A KILLER

...on the banks of a swift and treacherous river flowing through a narrow gorge, is a buried treasure, the stolen money gained by Bulldog Kelly in a hold-up that went wildly awry.

He started as a simple drifter blown north across the boundary line of the U.S. into the vast unprotected land called the Dominion of Canada. But when killing became his game, and blood was spilled on soil of the British Empire, he put an immense strain on American and British relations in his bid to avoid the gallows.

Edward Kelly was no garden-variety vagabond, no common desperado with cowardly blood running through his veins. True, he was a thief and a cold-blooded killer, but he had the luck of the Irish on his side. He also had some very good friends in some very high places—certainly an advantage for a condemned man facing charges of brutally slaying a fellow American on foreign soil.

Known in the province of British Columbia as "Bulldog" Kelly, the red-haired American first graced the pages of police files around 1884 in a bloody altercation that saw one man dead near the town of Golden on the Kicking Horse River. There, on the banks of a swift and treacherous river flowing through a narrow gorge, is a buried treasure, the stolen money gained by Bulldog Kelly in a hold-up that went wildly awry.

On November 27, 1884, at a place where the Kicking Horse River converges with the famed Kootenay trail, three men were riding through the bush heading south towards Montana Territory. At the centre of the party was a man named Robert McGregor Baird. He was a liquor salesman for the company Eddy, Hammond & Co. out of Missoula, Montana and he was heading home after a good season of trading, his saddlebags bulging with almost $4500 worth of gold and hard currency.

In the lead to break trail for the others was a young blacksmith named Manvel (in one account he is called Manuel) Drainard. He had been hired to accompany Baird to the state line. A few paces behind in the hard-packed snow was another man, the second escort hired for the trip, a Metis guide and packer documented only by his given name, Harry.

Coming down from Cariboo country where a gold rush was in full swing, the men had spent the night at a roadhouse called the Hog Ranch some few miles out of Golden. They had hit the trail early as the first light of the morning cracked the leaden skies.

Just as the path widened and the three men were able to ride abreast, a shot rang out from a dense grove of spruce and fir trees to the left of the company. The sound, a sudden crack, shattered the stillness of the morning and sent birds fluttering from the trees. Baird made a single sound, a strangled groan, before slumping forward in his saddle. Blood dripped from his chest onto the pristine winter snow.

Startled, Drainard took flight. Digging his spurs into the flanks of his horse, his first thought was to get out of the range of fire. He galloped up the trail at full speed, leaving the dead man and the young packer in the midst of an ambush.

Harry, also startled, reacted in a totally different manner. He rode straight towards the gunfire. He had seen the shadow of a man in the trees and was determined to tackle the killer. A second slug from the ambusher's rifle stuck him at the waist, shattering his left hip. Trying to ignore the pain, he leaped from the saddle onto the unknown man.

The assailant was none other than Bulldog Kelly. His rifle had been knocked to the ground as Harry flung himself from the saddle, the two men engaging in hand-to-hand combat. Fists flew in the ensuing struggle but Harry soon found his strength waning. Still he wrestled on, each man desperate to reach the single weapon, a Winchester rifle perched precariously on the edge of the river bank.

The young packer couldn't keep up the fight. Harry's strength ebbed by the second and he soon slumped into unconsciousness, a dead weight in Kelly's arms. Convinced his attacker was dead, Kelly reached for his rifle to finish the job, but accidentally knocked it over the embankment. He heard a splash below. Without a rifle at hand, Kelly settled on a few swift kicks to the head of the fallen man who was bleeding and comatose in the snow. That should finish him off.

Recovering enough to survey the scene, Kelly noted two men, one dead, one dying, and two horses milling about. He spied the coveted saddlebags on Baird's bay pony. With a smile, Kelly cut the pouches and fingered the loot that lay below the leather. He knew he was a rich man. But, with one of the three men gone, he also knew the authorities would soon be upon him. Best to be far away from this place, and carry no evidence.

At this point, it is widely held that Bulldog Kelly buried the saddle bags in a marked spot only he would know. Somewhere, it's maintained, about twenty-four miles south of the town of Golden, is the stashed earnings of a whiskey trader—gold currently valued at well over a million dollars.

Bulldog Kelly hid the money, and hit the trail on his horse at the same time young Drainard decided to turn back to check on his fallen comrades. By then Harry had regained consciousness. Weak and bleeding, he mounted Baird's horse and headed back to the Canadian Pacific construction camp on the Kicking Horse. He was the first to report the ambush and the whereabouts of Baird's stripped and broken body back in the bush. Whoever the attacker was had taken most of the clothing from the corpse—and Harry was thought it was the man known as Bulldog Kelly.

Kelly had been looking for something on the trader, and Harry knew that thing was gold. He had somehow survived the plunder of a gold-hungry highwayman and was witness to the fact. Reaching the camp shortly before nightfall, Harry told his grisly tale to the authorities who quickly mounted a posse to pursue the murderer.

Meanwhile, Drainard had come back to the murder site to find Baird dead and Harry gone. He rode to Golden to report the killing and soon the North-West Mounted Police and the Provincial Police, along with a militant group of angry railway construction workers, were united in the search for the killer Bulldog. A manhunt was on in some of the toughest country in British Columbia.

Police had heard of Kelly before. He was a loud-mouthed American braggart of no fixed address, who had been drifting around the Kootenay district for a year. He was known as a hot-headed fellow, and had striking red hair as befitted his Irish heritage. Word had spread that Bulldog Kelly was not someone you wanted to tangle with. The unprovoked murder of Baird re-reinforced the message that Kelly was a brutally dangerous man.

While the relentless posse combed hills and valleys in the mountainous Kicking Horse River and Golden areas, word of the murder spread across the prairies. From Winnipeg to Montana, posters of Kelly were distributed to North-West Mounted Police barracks and police detachments, sheriffs' offices and jailhouses.

The Montana company that employed Baird put up a $1000 reward to which the province immediately added $250. Yet Bulldog Kelly seemed to have vanished. His rifle, retrieved from the shallows of the Kicking Horse River at the scene of the crime, was the best evidence police had, but no clues to his whereabouts could be found. The trail was as cold as the fast approaching mid-winter freeze.

After a week of all-out searching, the manhunt dwindled. Volunteer trackers, hoping to get a share of the reward money, went back to their jobs. Only the police remained persistent in their search. A murderer was on the loose and there would be no rest until he was turned over to a court of law. Frontier justice needed to be served if the province was to avoid falling to the wild ways of its southern neighbour.

A sighting of Kelly in Golden, eight days after the murder, revived the hunt momentarily but a thorough search of the bars and bawdy houses of the frontier town proved futile. It appeared as though the outlaw had made good his escape to the American side of the line.

Fortunately, almost by fluke, a Provincial Police officer thought to check the eastbound train heading through Golden to Winnipeg, Manitoba. He wired ahead to a water stop down the line and asked the crew to check if any passengers could be described as five foot, eleven inches, blue-eyed, reddish hair and moustache, with a ruddy complexion.

Two NWMP officers happened to be onboard the train many hours later when the crew received the request. Knowing it to be a police matter, the second engineer brought the request for a search to the attention of Colonels A.G. Irvine and Macleod, who had spotted Kelly earlier but did not know he was linked to the British Columbia killing.

Irvine was the first to approach Kelly who was standing by a window watching the endless prairie grassland roll by. He passed by once to double-check his identification, and when he turned the red-haired man stepped to the platform between coaches. Without wasting a moment, Irvine approached him directly. As he was about to utter the words, "You're under arrest," Kelly leaped from the slow-moving train. Before the eyes of the astonished Irvine, the bandit rolled twice, regained his footing, then ran across the prairie to a parcel of trees.

Hauling on the emergency chord, Irvine signaled the engineer to stop. By the time the great iron beast had come wheezing and shuddering to a halt, the Mounties were a good mile from the spot Kelly had landed. They rushed back down the track and quickly scoured the plains, but could find no sign of the bandit. The best they could do was report his disappearance to all detachments of the NWMP from the next station. The CPR line near Winnipeg runs close to the border, and after a thorough search of the area, police could only conclude that Kelly had managed to get across the line to the United States.

Months passed and in early spring 1885, Bulldog Kelly surfaced again. It is here that accounts of his fugitive days differ. Some historians claim he was captured in a small town in Dakota Territory by Minnesota authorities while others claim he was arrested near St. Paul, Minnesota by Special Constable Jack Kirkup of Revelstoke, B.C. Regardless of what city he was captured in, the fact that Kelly was wanted in Canada meant an extradition hearing, and final justice for the slain Baird. It was not to be.

While an American judicial commissioner ruled that Kelly, who also went by the name Edward Laughlin, should be returned to Canada, some string-pulling at different levels of government saw that ruling overturned.

Kelly, it proved, was a Fenian, an Irish terrorist organization intent on overthrowing British dominance in the New World. His Irish heritage worked strongly in his favour. The Fenians managed to delay the extradition and started a legal defence fund for Kelly. There was no way they were going to hand over one of their own to the malevolent British justice system, which would rather hang an Irishman than give him the time of day.

Canadian officials, namely Deputy Attorney General Paulus Aemilius Irving and his colleagues in government, were dumbfounded. An American had been killed by another American in cold blood. The crime had been committed on Canadian soil. Witnesses were available, the evidence was in and the charges irrefutable. Why were the Americans harbouring a known felon when justice under British rule was certain?

Kelly's American lawyer "Big Tom" Ryan had whispered the answer to Irving's question into the ear of Secretary of State Thomas Bayard. And the answer was political—election votes.

Millions of people of Irish descent would withhold their political favours if an Irishman was delivered to the hands of the blood-hungry Brits in Canada. Ryan insisted that Kelly's betrayal at the hands of his own government would cost Democratic President Grover Cleveland many, many Irish votes.

The American media got hold of the story and Baird's murder on the far-away Kicking Horse River was all but forgotten. Handing over Kelly to the Canadians became a political hot potato and eventually, despite protests from Ottawa, Bulldog Kelly was set free.

With the extradition order quashed by the Americans, relations between the two countries became extremely strained. Editorials in both the Victoria newspaper and the St. Paul newspaper railed against each other.

An editorial writer for the *Victoria Colonist* said:

"Money and political influences have been too potent, and Kelly is now treading the firm soil and breathing the pure air of a country where all are free—free to make justice a travesty, to treat murder as a joke and to turn a criminal trial and sentence into a mockery. ...

"Kelly may be legally free, but he goes forth with a red stain on his conscience, if he has any, and with a liberty that is conditional upon his never placing his feet upon British soil. Until then, his crime rests between himself and his Maker. As it is, the U.S. is responsible...for prostituting its freedom by wrapping its flag around the body of a prima facie murderer. ..."

In response, *St. Paul's Irish Standard* was equally, if not more, scathing. It read:

"Kelly the accused, remained for a considerable time in the northwest after the murder, unmolested, and it was not until he had crossed the line into the U.S. that the bloodhounds of the so-called British justice, true to the instincts of their bloodthirsty ancestors, came in pursuit, endeavoring to trample down every vestige of justice and fair play in our midst, and drag the object of their enmity again into their kennels and consign him as many an honest Irishman has been consigned before, to an ignominious death on the scaffold whose bloodstains, like the blood of Abel, cry aloud for vengeance on the cowardly curs who have so often besmeared it with the heart's blood of the bravest and true. The Canadian government has already spent $30,000 on the case through the instrumentality of a corduroyed, tight pants dude of a lawyer they sent here, who knew well that the guilty party was not Kelly."

The vitriol between the borders was a palpable thing but, as Bulldog Kelly drifted into anonymity, so too did the animosity between Canada and the States eventually die down.

The saga of Bulldog Kelly has a gruesome if not just ending, and fortunately, the murderer did not live long enough to realize the profits of his stolen goods. Less than three years after his extradition was quashed, Kelly was working as a brakeman on the Northern Pacific Railway.

The caboose driver on that line recalled Kelly telling him it was his last trip. At the station—the train was bound for Helena, Montana—Kelly was planning to pack it in and head back north to British Columbia.

"Enough time has passed now," said Kelly to his colleague, with a swift wink. "I'm coming into some money north of the border and I aim to retire." Little did the murderer know the Helena run, that April afternoon of 1890, was truly his last.

As the train pulled into the station, Kelly slipped while running to his post. He fell between the train cars and both legs were crushed and almost severed by the wheels. He died on a Helena operating table with his stolen booty—his retirement package, the money he so callously stripped from the still-warm body of Robert McGregor Baird—buried on a rugged hillside somewhere near the raging Kicking Horse River. Many believe it is still there.

FORT QU'APPELLE, 1880s

8

RACETTE AND GADDY: PORTRAIT OF A DEADLY DUO

*Unbeknownst to them, in an act of pure vanity,
Moise Racette and James Gaddy had posed
for their own "Wanted" poster.*

here is a certain brotherhood among outlaws and, it could be said, a certain pride. As a man who lives his life to the letter of the law with no deviation feels some conceit, so do men of the criminal element. Horse-rustling, hold-ups, the terror on the faces of those being robbed or brutalized—these can become the stuff of bar-room bragging, stars in the crowns of cowards who live by brawn and bravado backed by a trigger-happy finger.

This scenario was the case of two young ex-convicts who met by chance at a saloon in Wolseley, in what is now Saskatchewan, in the spring of 1887. They reminisced about their days in the Stony Mountain Penitentiary just north of Winnipeg. The two men didn't know each other from their prison days, but they most certainly had mutual friends who were still behind jail walls. While sipping whiskey in a public house, it must have been easy to romanticize the lock-up and the exploits that put them behind bars.

With the sun shining and a haze of spring green on all the fields, twenty-six-year-old Moise Racette bragged to his younger drinking partner about the property his family owned just north of Wolseley and about the two years he served for horse theft. He had just been released from "The Pen," as it was referred to by inmates, and he filled his new friend in on the comings and goings at Stony.

James Gaddy, twenty-two, had been out of prison since 1884, released early for good behaviour. But his two years outside of prison had not proved as bountiful as young Gaddy had anticipated. Trouble plagued him, it seemed. Gaddy was constantly in trouble with police, who prowled the Crooked Lake reserve where he lived, and his wife of less than a year had recently indicated she had no interest in continuing to live with him.

Racette, embracing his new-found freedom, seemed to have better prospects than Gaddy. As they polished off a bottle of whiskey between them, an easy friendship sprang up. They would go together to Racette's place where his father would provide shelter and odd jobs, it was decided.

From there, the future was wide open.

It didn't take long for the two friends to decide a life of lawlessness was a simpler and smoother path than the straight-and-narrow road of farm labouring. Living by the law demanded too much hard work and despite the strength of youth and stocky, well-muscled bodies, Racette and Gaddy determined to forsake the farm for the quick take of thieves.

A few miles southeast of Wolseley in Fort Qu'Appelle, the men bought guns to furnish their new lifestyle and to celebrate the purchase that would earn them a living, they stopped at the makeshift tent studio of travelling Winnipeg portrait photographer Allen Sutherland.

"Let's get our photo took," said Racette, squinting his eyes so they almost disappeared beneath thick, menacing eyebrows.

"We're startin' out, ain't we," agreed Gaddy, the less confident of the two. "Might as well."

And so they ducked into the canvas doorway of Sutherland's studio for a formal sitting. While Sutherland arranged the large plates and draped the black cloth over his head, Racette made uncannily prophetic jokes about the hangman and the dark hood that would eventually cover his own head.

When the prints were ready, neither had the cost of the paper in their pockets. Realizing he was being stiffed, Sutherland refused to give the rowdy customers their image. The men went away empty handed, not realizing that same photo would soon grace every North-West Mounted Police (NWMP) barracks in the region as well as a good number of police posts in Dakota and Montana territories. Unbeknownst to them, in an act of pure vanity, Moise Racette and James Gaddy had posed for their own "Wanted" poster. It was one of Fate's little laughs.

By the end of May 1887, the troublesome duo had jumped a freight car to Moose Jaw and had helped themselves to three good-looking horses they'd seen corralled east of the settlement. Newly mounted and giddy with their first heist, the boys got greedy. They were planning to head back to

Wolseley, via Fort Qu'Appelle, to show off their new ponies, but changed their minds, thinking they'd might as well snag another horse en route. That way, they reasoned, they'd each have one to ride and one to sell. A little pocket money and maybe the barrel of a gun might be just the encouragement the cocky photographer from Fort Qu'Appelle needed in order to hand over their pictures.

The fourth horse was liberated from the back paddock of Scottish settler Hector McLeish on May 29. The next morning Gaddy and Racette were being tracked by McLeish and his neighbour J.R. Brown, neither of whom could abide horse thieves. At Fort Qu'Appelle McLeish and Brown enlisted the help of NWMP Sergeant John Tyffe and a posse of other men intent on quelling rampant theft in the area.

The posse split into two parties and soon it was evident that the horse rustlers were heading to Wolseley. Homesteaders in the area positively identified Racette as one of the outlaws and a quick conference was convened with local NWMP officer Donald Mathewson. Because the Racette place was less than a mile out of town, most of the men decided to put up in the Wolseley Hotel. McLeish and Mathewson, however, decided they should carry on to the outlaw's homestead to confront the felon and his accomplice.

It should have been a simple arrest but when backed into a corner, convicts tend to fight. That's exactly what happened at the Racette ranch in the final evening hours of May 30, 1887.

Mathewson and McLeish stationed themselves outside the ramshackle farmhouse waiting for one of the fugitives to appear. They didn't wait long. Moise Racette came out on the porch and headed across the yard to a barn where a number of horses were tied outside. As Racette was readying the tack, Mathewson stepped up behind him and, placing a hand on his wrist, uttered the words least favoured by fugitives: "You're under arrest."

Racette whirled around, a cry of surprise dying on his lips as he looked into the eyes of the police officer. He seemed ready to surrender but for the advance of his buddy James Gaddy.

Gaddy was unaware of what was taking place in the yard when he stepped off the porch to assist Racette in saddling the horses to make good their escape. As McLeish went forward to capture young James Gaddy, Racette's father slipped through the farmhouse door. While McLeish laid his hands on Gaddy, the senior Racette jumped McLeish from behind, assuming he and his son had caught some horse thieves redhanded.

Gaddy jerked free from McLeish and grabbed for the revolver that had been knocked out of McLeish's hand when the senior Racette joined in the tussle. Without a moment's hesitation the young man let go three shots. One hit McLeish in the arm, the next in the side, causing him to spin around, and as he sunk to the ground, the final bullet entered his back. The rancher would see only one more dawn before the eternal night fell.

The wounding of McLeish seemed to subdue everyone. As Mathewson and the elder Racette carried him into the cabin, the two outlaws remained outside hatching another desperate and somewhat pathetic killing scheme. They had to get rid of Mathewson before he took the news back to town, but, both cowardly, neither men was willing to shoot him outright. They would kill him, yes, but not while looking him in the eye. Neither man, it seemed, had the appetite for a cold-blooded murder.

A plan was laid to shoot him from afar. While Moise Racette walked towards town, ostensibly to get a doctor for McLeish, James Gaddy would lie await in the ditch. An abrupt whistle would be the signal for Racette to dive to the road, allowing Gaddy the opportunity to shoot the police officer. So it was decided.

And so, too, it would have happened had not the bright moon cast long shadows in the trees. With a light wind blowing the trees, shadows danced across the road, making the target appear to sway and waiver in the darkness. Hearing Racette's whistle, Gaddy fired his shot but missed Mathewson. The officer knew he was being ambushed and, hoping the bullets would stop, he plastered himself against Racette. The ploy worked. Gaddy let off two more shots, both near misses, but held fire when he could no longer discern one man from the other. He didn't want to accidentally kill his friend.

For reasons unknown, Racette and Gaddy again chose not to kill Mathewson and the three backtracked for the farm. Warning the NWMP officer to stay indoors with Moise's father and the wounded settler, the two bandits saddled their horses and rode off into the night.

A faint gurgle from the lips of McLeish stirred Mathewson. He took a horse and rode quickly to town to summon Doc Hutchinson from his bed. By the time a wagon was rigged and the wounded Scotsman was moved back to town, it was too late. McLeish died of his wounds at around 8 a.m. The two fugitives were no longer simple horse thieves—now they were murderers.

While a large posse of men combed the Crooked Lake reserve where Gaddy's relatives lived, the two men hightailed it south towards the American border. They rode by night and hid by day, avoiding contact with people as much as possible in order to make good their escape. Across the prairie, Gaddy and Racette rode, until they crossed the line into Montana Territory.

Finally free of Canadian authority, both men assumed different identities to preserve their freedom. But the Fort Qu'Appelle portrait in the hands of the unpaid photographer came back to haunt them and, like winter snow, it spread their likeness across the plains.

Allen Sutherland, the photographer, was back in Winnipeg reading the June 2 edition of the *Manitoba Free Press* when he came across an item that grabbed his attention. It was about McLeish's death in Wolseley, and the article contained a detailed description of the killers. The picture that sprang to his mind was of the two brutish fellows who had glowered at his camera a month earlier.

Unable to shake his hunch, Sutherland sent the unclaimed photo to Lieutenant-Governor Edgar Dewdney in Regina, who had the men positively identified as the two desperadoes Gaddy and Racette. He ordered copies of the photograph and distributed them to NWMP barracks south of Regina. The officers there passed the posters on to Indian agents and U.S. sheriffs south of the border and on July 18, the bandits were spotted outside of Fort Ellice near what is now the Manitoba-Saskatchewan border.

Somehow the outlaws got wind of an approaching posse, and for the first time in their unholy alliance, Gaddy and Racette split up, effectively covering their tracks. But capture was not far off. On August 12, a county sheriff in Lewiston, Montana, recognized the two strangers hanging about the army post of Fort McGinnis as Gaddy and Racette. He'd seen their photograph and it was enough to convince him to carry on with an arrest.

There was jubilation in NWMP headquarters in Regina when they heard the twosome had been captured. A trio of men, including officer Mathewson, who had subsequently obtained the rank of corporal, rode down to Montana to bring the criminals back to Canada.

By November, extradition hearings were complete and Gaddy and Racette were imprisoned in the NWMP head-quarters in Regina. The shadow of the noose hung over them for nine long weeks as their defence lawyer argued that James Gaddy had not been of sound mind when he fired the shots that killed McLeish.

The facts, however, spoke for themselves, and the Crown felt it had a fairly tight case. Justice Edward Ludlow Wetmore and a jury of six impartial men agreed Gaddy and Racette were culpable in the crime. They were convicted of murdering Hector McLeish and in February both men were sentenced to be hanged.

The day of the hanging dawned bright and clear. It was June 13, 1888, just over a year since the team had hooked up in Wolseley's public house. James Gaddy and Moise Racette were led from their cells to the scaffold in the barracks at Regina, the same yard that had seen Louis Riel hanged three years earlier.

Before they climbed the stairs to the gallows, however, they paused in the yard to do one last thing. A man with a black cloth over his head bent low and snapped a final photograph of the doomed pair. Their last portrait is vastly different from their first. No longer are two cocky, confident criminals grinning out from the frame. This time, in their last moments on earth, Gaddy and Racette look death squarely in the eyes.

They do not smile.

CHARCOAL

9

CHARCOAL: ONE MAN AGAINST THE MULTITUDE

He could be in one place one day, and the next day, a hundred miles away. Tracking the Indian was like tracking a spirit, so familiar was he with the landscape and so easily able to find and help himself to fresh horses.

In the lore and tradition of the once-mighty Plains Indians there is a belief that your status as a brave will be maintained in the "Land of the Dead" as long as one person precedes you. That person should be one of your worst enemies, hastened into Death by the deed of great courage—a killing. If this enemy dies before you and by your hand, he will herald you into the "Land of the Dead" and your status as a warrior will go undiminished.

Such was the conviction of Si'-okskitsis, a Blood Indian of legendary strength and cunning who lived with his tribe along the Belly River in southwestern Alberta in the later part of the nineteenth century. By the time the first North-West Mounted Police (NWMP) battalion reached Alberta in 1874 rumours of Si'-okskitsis, the Indian locally known as Charcoal, had already reached them. Somewhere beyond the forts and barracks erected in the small settlements of Fort Macleod in the north, Cardston in the south and Pincher Creek in the west lived a warrior of great repute who was feared and admired by the Cree, the Kootenay, the Assiniboine and the Crow.

Charcoal's reputation of power and bravery was not lost on the police. But it seemed impossible that the two could meet without a resounding clash. And when destiny was finally fulfilled, when the NWMP and Charcoal engaged in a battle of wits and cunning, a chain of events unravelled that would eventually see Charcoal heralded into the "Land of the Dead" by an NWMP officer, slain after a two-month chase.

Charcoal was a renegade from birth. Son of a renowned warrior, he was born sometime around 1841 and grew up in a small clan called the Shooting-Up band. Perhaps the most feared of the Blood Indians, this group distinguished themselves by raiding neighbouring tribes and stealing their most coveted possession—horses.

In his lifetime Charcoal was a witness to the great decline of the Blood people. He saw the arrival of the white man and watched epidemics such as smallpox and tuberculosis spread and kill his people like flies. He also witnessed the slaughter of great herds of buffalo. He was one of a determined group of Blood Indians who refused to attend the signing of the Blackfoot Crossing Treaty No. 7 in 1877, where the natives were convinced to give up their rights to a nomadic life in exchange for reserves. Charcoal and a band of non-treaty Blood retreated to the south across the border into Montana Territory, rather than submit to the rule that insisted on penning a proud people behind invisible lines.

In 1896 Charcoal became defiant, insisting he live his life according to the laws of his own people. He became an outlaw after a cold-blooded killing, which in his ancient tradition sparked the demand he take at least one of his enemies with him into the next world.

An unfaithful wife with a wandering eye was the beginning of Charcoal's undoing. While his strength and agility still brought him status among his people, his wife brought him great dishonour. It was reasoned that if a man could not keep his own wife in line, he was not worthy of respect.

Pretty Wolverine Woman, Charcoal's fourth wife, was enamoured with her cousin Medicine Pipe Stem. She would probably have been prepared to love her cousin from afar had it not been for the unannounced arrival of eighteen-year-old Sleeping Woman to the conjugal tipi. Sleeping Woman was Charcoal's chosen fifth wife. While polygamy was totally accepted among the Blood Indians, the unwritten rules prevailed: all wives must live happily with one man. Should a wife look elsewhere for affection, shame is brought on the head of the husband.

In September 1896 the mounting attraction between Wolverine Woman and Medicine Pipe Stem was apparent. At a hay cut near the reserve, Charcoal noticed his fourth wife and her cousin had disappeared. He followed them to a shed where he found them in the throes of passionate lovemaking. Charcoal felt there was no choice. He had been publicly humiliated by his wife and a young brave well-known in the Blood community. If word got out that the two had become lovers, he would be a laughing stock, his status sadly diminished.

Taking his rifle, Charcoal calmly walked into the shed and put a single bullet into Medicine Pipe Stem's left eye. The bullet travelled directly into the young man's brain, killing him instantly. Satisfied with the quick kill, Charcoal took his horrified wife's hand, and after gently closing the eyelid over the bullet hole in her lover's face, they made their way back to the Blood reserve.

The corpse wasn't discovered until ten days later when a group of young Blood women where out looking for firewood. Word of the grisly discovery soon filtered into the NWMP detachment at nearby Pincher Creek, and a coroner was dispatched to the site on October 10, 1896. While the dead Indian caused eyebrows to raise in certain detachments around the area, a second less serious incident was what really stirred the NWMP into action.

On the evening of October 12, government Indian agent Edward McNeil sat by his coal lamp and prepared to write a report. He had been hired by the government to teach the natives cattle farming, necessary now that buffalo were almost completely gone from the great prairie. Transforming hunters to gatherers was no easy task and McNeil was not particularly popular among the Blood and Peigan and he was actively disliked by a smaller group of natives—including the defiant Charcoal—who held him responsible for their drastic change in lifestyle.

Little did McNeil know as he sat, pen poised, that Charcoal was crouched outside his window. He had been selected as one of the enemy, one of a handful of people who could secure a native man's status in the sacred Sandhills of eternity. Knowing his time on earth was limited after the murder of Medicine Pipe Stem, Charcoal proceeded with his plan. As McNeil stood, Charcoal fired. Shooting wide, the bullet only grazed McNeil's arm, but by the time he staggered to the window in an effort to identify his assailant, the shooter had disappeared into the night. McNeil had no idea who shot at him. Or why.

That evening Charcoal gathered his family around him and told them they had no option but to flee. The banished party consisted of women and children: two of Charcoal's wives, his mother-in-law, a daughter, and two stepsons, ten-year-old Bear's Head, and a young, unnamed boy. With tipis and supplies in tow, the band headed southwest across the plains towards the Rocky Mountains. Charcoal, supposing McNeil dead, was running from the law and taking his family with him. It was a cumbersome group.

Word quickly spread through the Blood lodges that Charcoal had gone mad. He was on a killing spree, it was rumoured. No one was safe.

North-West Mounted Police Superintendent Sam Steele, stationed in Fort Macleod, took a personal interest in the hunt for the fugitive and his family. On October 15, 1896, Steele issued a warrant for Charcoal's arrest and organized a search party to pursue the outlaw.

His motive for wanting the native brought to justice had as much to do with politics as it did with Steele's reputation as a man who would abide no lawlessness. In Ottawa, Sir Wilfrid Laurier and his Liberal party had been elected to power. Part of their mandate was to examine—and possibly disband—the North-West Mounted Police force in light of "Indian troubles." Steele, who cut a powerful figure, would do everything in his power to make sure this did not happen. The NWMP had become his own police force and he wanted to ensure its authority. Capturing Charcoal would put an end to the rumours of "Indian troubles" in his part of the country and quell the eastern suspicions that the NWMP weren't doing their job.

While another massive search was underway in the northern part of what is now Alberta and Saskatchewan (see Almighty Voice, chapter 10) Steele wanted to make sure his territory was solidly ruled by Mountie authority. No full-breed renegade Indian with funny ideas about a traditional way of life and native justice was going to get away with cold-blooded killing and firing pot shots at whomever he pleased. Steele, with his Mounties and their maxim to "always get their man," was determined to bring Charcoal into Fort Macleod and string him up for murder.

In mid-October, Steele and his men discovered Charcoal and his family across the U.S. border in what is now Glacier National Park. They had established a camp in the woods at the foot of Chief Mountain and seemed quite settled. Ponies milled about, campfires had been smothered and two tipis were standing in a sandy hollow.

On October 17, the Mounties decided to close in. Led by NWMP officer A.M. Jarvis, the posse crept towards the camp, trying to remain silent in the still morning. Reports say the officers went as far as removing their shoes to avoid detection. The crack of a dry twig alerted Charcoal to the intruders and gunfire was exchanged. Again, reports vary as to who fired first. Some say Charcoal let off a single shot before disappearing inside a tipi. Other reports claim the NWMP were so anxious to get their man that they fired wildly and randomly at the camp. A bullet grazed the top of Jarvis' head, but it is just as likely it was from his own men as it was from Charcoal's rifle.

The police descended and captured three of the seven fugitives. Charcoal's mother-in-law, his daughter and the smallest boy were taken into custody along with a cache of food and ammunition. But the prized capture was long gone, having vanished into the hills with his two wives and his stepsons in tow.

Word went back to the barracks for reinforcement and a second contingent of NWMP, led by Inspector Henry Davidson, arrived to surround the area. With the help of some Blood mercenaries, the officers made a human chain around the mountain valley. Sure that Charcoal and company were within the boundaries, they planned to go in on foot the next morning, closing the circle and capturing the family like flies in the centre of a shrinking web.

Perhaps the Blood were less faithful than the Mounties assumed. Perhaps they let their brother slip past them. Whatever the case, Charcoal was not found that night nor the next. In fact, the legendary Charcoal outsmarted them all when a report came to Inspector Jarvis that two police horses, stabled overnight in a ranch nearby on the Oldman River, had disappeared. Charcoal and his entourage had slipped through the night and stolen fresh horses from under the noses of the men intent on his capture.

Sam Steele was angry. His resolve to see Charcoal pay for his crimes strengthened with this last NWMP humiliation. Posting a $200 reward, Steele gathered anyone he could find, any reasonable man, cowboy, rancher or Indian recruit, and armed them with police rifles in order to take up the chase.

One of the men who gladly received the call to arms was Sergeant William Brock Wilde from the NWMP Pincher Creek detachment. A veteran of the Royal Irish Dragoon Guard, Wilde had fourteen years in the mounted corps under his belt. He was one of the toughest men on the force, afraid of nothing, and had little or no respect for Indians. In his mind, a good Indian was a dead Indian, and he was the man who wanted to make Charcoal good and dead. He joined the search party and soon became the second man intent on putting Charcoal in his rightful place: the scaffold, followed closely by the grave.

After leaving a false trail into the Montana wilderness, Charcoal had doubled back on his tracks and was heading north to the Porcupine Hills. Somewhat short of supplies he was forced to stop near the banks of the Oldman River where he set up a make-shift camp and proceeded to raid the nearest house, that of Metis settler Mose Legrandeur. After taking the man's food and two horses from the nearby Peigan reserve, Charcoal resumed his journey. But his trail was now marked and the police were in hot pursuit. Somehow, between Legrandeur's place and the Oldman River, Charcoal vanished.

By the end of October snow was falling on the plains. With winter setting in, the NWMP tired of the chase. Steele heard rumours of Charcoal but nothing seemed to result in a sure sighting of the man. At the same time, newspapers were beginning to become quite critical of the police force, publicly declaring it ineffectual. Steele was getting more and more agitated. The search for the killer had gone on too long already.

Out in the elements, Charcoal had his own problems. His wives, sick of being on the run, were fighting among themselves and threatening to expose him to the law. At a camp in the foothills near Dry Forks, Charcoal resorted to violence to keep his family loyal. After abandoning young Bear's Head on the Peigan reserve, Charcoal tied Sleeping Woman and Wolverine Woman back to back, so they wouldn't escape. Leaving the two women in a tipi, he headed for his brother's camp on the Blood reserve.

Certain their husband would return to kill them, the women escaped by chewing through the ropes on their hands. They fled in fear, following the river south towards home. Charcoal wouldn't let his women go easily, however, and after returning from a midnight horse and supply raid on the

Blood reserve, he tracked them, intent on bringing them back. The pursued had suddenly become the pursuer.

Forced to hide in an abandoned beaver lodge, the women escaped detection but were terrified by the experience. They later told the NWMP officers who seized them that Charcoal had walked through the bush calling out to them. His words were chilling. Sleeping Woman would be spared, he chanted, because it was Wolverine Woman who had initially caused all the trouble. He was willing to kill one wife in order to get the other back.

Without the burden of his family, Charcoal's movements became even more difficult to follow. Police were amazed at his flight. He could be in one place one day, and the next day, 100 miles away. Tracking the Indian was like tracking a spirit, so familiar was he with the landscape and so easily able to find and help himself to fresh horses.

So the hunt continued: 100 armed men searching up and down the Oldman River, through the coulees of the Porcupine Hills, at the headwaters of the Belly River, seeking an elusive outlaw Indian who refused capture. And the snow continued to fall.

It wasn't until November 2 at the Mounted Police detachment in Cardston, on the southwest border of the Peigan reserve, that Charcoal surfaced again. Just before nightfall, as a young officer, Corporal William Armer, stepped out of the barracks to check a disturbance in the paddock, a shot was fired. Charcoal's bullet—or at least a bullet whose caliber matched that of the slug taken from the head of Medicine Pipe Stem—passed between Armer's upper arm and chest, narrowly missing his heart. There was something desperate about the shooting and police were puzzled at Charcoal's seemingly random choice of victims.

Meanwhile, in local settlements and on the Blood reserve, Charcoal's relatives were rounded up like cattle. Charcoal's brother Left Hand and his huge extended family were brought into Fort Macleod and charged with aiding and abetting a criminal because word had reached police about Charcoal's midnight visit to the Blood reserve.

Left Hand was suspect, and for good measure, Charcoal's other brother Bear's Back Bone was also arrested. It was this random and threatening act of coersion that could have been what prompted the attack at Cardston, but at this point police intended to use any tactics they could to bring the fugitive to justice.

With his infant son ill, the imprisoned Left Hand was under growing pressure to agree to Sam Steele's latest plan to lure Charcoal home. The police believed Charcoal would eventually have to find shelter with his relatives. They struck a deal with the imprisoned people: you help us bring Charcoal in and we set you free. No help, and charges of assisting a criminal would be pressed.

Bear's Back Bone and Left Hand had few options. They agreed to help the red coats capture their brother. Dipping into the reserve of horses on either Blood or Peigan land, Charcoal was constantly on the move, keeping trackers baffled as to his whereabouts.

Sergeant William Brock Wilde was the man in charge of the posse that finally tracked Charcoal down, near Dry Forks, on the northern tributary of the Kootenay River. Heavy snow was falling, discouraging the party of Indian scouts and ranchers Wilde had armed for the hunt.

As they mounted a hill, the posse spotted Charcoal at a distance of some 300 feet. Charcoal was on a horse and was leading another. As soon as the posse moved towards him, Charcoal changed ponies, letting the unsaddled horse run free. Wilde knew the Indian had the advantage with the fresh horse. He and his men had just plowed through thirty miles of snow and everyone in the party was exhausted. But the prey was so close. Wilde could see him clearly, and the legendary Charcoal had never looked as pretty as he did down the barrel of Wilde's rifle.

While most of the men dismounted on the crest of the hill, Wilde pressed on, intent on getting the outlaw now so close at hand. With just minutes between them, Wilde rode forward, rifle at his side and his revolver in hand.

Charcoal also rode on, patiently waiting while the gap between the men closed. When Charcoal estimated Wilde was within range, the wait was over. He turned abruptly in his saddle. This wild white man would do as well as any. Placing his rifle firmly against his shoulder, Charcoal aimed and fired at the pursuant officer. The bullet struck Wilde in the side knocking him to the snow. Wheeling his mount, Charcoal came abreast of Wilde and, with a blood curdling war-whoop, put a final bullet in his body. The white man would be his ticket to the hereafter. The deed was done.

Charcoal galloped away leaving a shocked group of men. It seemed impossible that their leader would be the one to die and yet the evidence gazed up at them with lifeless eyes. Charcoal, after two failed attempts, had killed his second man.

Wilde's body was moved to Pincher Creek, and a hasty inquest was called. After a full military funeral for the fallen officer, the hunt for the killer resumed.

The police were ultimately correct in their assumption that a lone fugitive will always return home. On November 12, a timid knock came to the door of Left Hand's cabin on the Blood reserve. He opened the door to a gaunt, weary Charcoal. Exhausted from the relentless running, yet reluctant to give himself up, Charcoal had plowed through sixty miles of snow in order to return to his home.

His brothers weren't the only ones to greet the exhausted man, however. Police scouts had been stationed at both brothers' cabins and before Charcoal could get food in his belly or warmth in his fingers, the NWMP were on him.

Justice was hastily served. Within days of his capture, Charcoal was taken from the Fort Macleod guardhouse to be tried and convicted of the murders of Medicine Pipe Stem and Sergeant William Wilde. He was sentenced to be hanged March 16, 1897.

Bound and determined not to go the way of the white man Charcoal attempted suicide in prison, puncturing his wrists

FUNERAL PROCESSION FOR SERGEANT W.B. WILDE

with a moccasin awl. Equally determined to see him with a noose around his neck, prison guards kept him under close surveillance. When he refused to eat, they kept him alive by force feeding.

Superintendent Sam Steele expressed shock when he finally came face to face with Charcoal days before the execution. He was emaciated and suffering from terminal tuberculosis. Steele was amazed this small sack of flesh and blood was the man who had tortured and eluded the NWMP for over two months.

Charcoal was so weak by the time his death date arrived that he had to be carried to the gallows. Singing the Indian death song, the Blood brave fell to his death, anxious to regain his glorious warrior status in the next world.

ALMIGHTY VOICE

10

ALMIGHTY VOICE: THE LAST DEFIANT STAND

...he thumbed his nose at white man's authority and so began one of the prairie's longest, and bloodiest, manhunts in Saskatchewan's history.

In a grim semi-circle hundreds of Cree and Metis people stand on a bluff overlooking a large poplar grove. A woman begins to chant the Cree death lament. It goes on and on, a continuous wail, lost only occasionally in the roar of cannon fire as a large group of uniformed men lob shells into the patch of trees and dense bush below.

The woman is singing for her son, the legendary Almighty Voice, who, taking refuge in the stand of trees, will die that day, May 30, 1897. His will not be the only death on the prairies near the Minnichinas Hills, in what is now central Saskatchewan. By the time the cannons are silent and the last note of the death song is sung, seven men will be gone, three natives and four white men, felled in the struggle for authority that played itself out, time and time again, in the early days of the Canadian West.

The true tragedy of Almighty Voice is that the deaths could have so easily been prevented. As is usually the case in these matters, the initial conflict that escalated into an all-out battle, complete with two cannon and almost 100 North-West Mounted police officers, was small, almost incidental.

Almighty Voice, twenty-one years old, was originally arrested by NWMP officer Sergeant Colin Colebrook on October 22, 1895, for slaughtering an ownerless cow in June that same year. The young brave, who by all reports was strikingly handsome and a bit of a ladies' man, was preparing for a wedding feast—his fourth marriage, this time to a thirteen-year-old girl—when the cow wandered into his sights on the One Arrow reserve near Batoche. The cow solved an immediate problem for Almighty Voice. How many people could come to the feast was determined by what he could provide. The hapless cow quickly became steak for his guests.

There are mixed reports about ownership of the cow, a beast that perpetuated one of the most unsavoury battles on the prairies. Some say it was a government cow lent to the reserve for breeding purposes. Other authorities say the cow was likely a stray from a nearby ranch. Regardless of the cow's origin, Almighty Voice saw it as a gift for his wedding feast and the lone, wandering cow became meat for a tribe that, with the slaughter and loss of the buffalo some twenty years previously, had seen its share of starvation.

The incident would have gone completely unnoticed if it weren't for a former brother-in-law. The man mentioned the cow-butchering incident to an authority at Duck Lake—the young Constable Colebrook—and when Almighty Voice went to the settlement to collect his treaty money, he and a companion were arrested and put in jail.

It's impossible to know what went through the mind of Almighty Voice that night he spent in the white man's jail, but he may have ruminated on his grandfather's three-year prison stint following the 1885 North-West Rebellion a decade earlier. Almighty Voice grew up with tales of how his father, John Sounding Sky, and his father's father, One Arrow, Chief of the Swampy Cree, had banded with other Metis and Indians under Gabriel Dumont at Batoche to fight the forces from Eastern Canada. The Rebellion ended in a massive defeat and not only were the Swampy Cree deprived of their chief, but One Arrow was deprived of his freedom and put behind bars for his part in the uprising.

Another prison incident surely played in the mind of Almighty Voice as he sat in the Duck Lake lock-up. His father, John Sounding Sky, had been arrested three days earlier on charges of theft. He was given a six-month sentence and sent to Prince Albert. Rumours had drifted back to the reserve that their one-time leader was now shovelling manure for the NWMP. Fearing the same fate, Almighty Voice, whose Cree name was Kisse-manitou-wayo but appeared on the agency records as Jean Baptiste, waited until the prison guards changed shifts. In the early hours of October 23, 1895, he simply walked out the unlocked door of the Duck Lake prison. In doing so, he thumbed his nose at white man's authority and so began one of the prairie's longest, and bloodiest manhunts.

Free in the prairie night, Almighty Voice hightailed it from town to the South Saskatchewan River, almost five miles east of the Duck Lake settlement. Despite freezing water, he plunged into the river around Batoche Crossing and swam to the other side. Heading deep into One Arrow's reserve,

Almighty Voice rested briefly at his mother Spotted Calf's home and then carried on northeast to the John Smith reserve at Fort a La Corne where his new bride awaited him.

Meanwhile, police, unnerved that the prisoner had walked away from them, were paying surprise visits to the relatives of Almighty Voice. With their authority threatened, it was suddenly paramount that Almighty Voice yield to the law imposed by the Queen's representatives. If he was left to roam, it would undermine the NWMP mandate to maintain order in the land.

The natives at the One Arrow reserve were mute, however, when asked about their own. Yes Almighty Voice had been there, but yes he had disappeared.

A full week after the prison break, Sergeant Colin Colebrook and his Metis guide and interpreter François Dumont finally got a tip, again from the family of a slighted ex-wife. Almighty Voice and his wife were tracked thirty miles from the Batoche Crossing to their camp, just south of Kinistino on October 29.

Officer Colebrook rode boldly towards the camp. He asked his interpreter to tell Almighty Voice to surrender, thinking there would be no protest; after all, his command was law. He rode in, deaf to the words of the translator and oblivious to Almighty Voice's threatening actions.

Hoisting his rifle to his shoulder and aiming it squarely at the approaching police officer, Almighty Voice spoke in Cree: "Leave us. I must kill you if you don't turn back."

The message, clear as a prairie morning, was translated by Dumont.

"He's serious," Dumont added in English, urgently concerned that Colebrook understand he was in danger.

Again the message came from Almighty Voice who had stepped in front of his wife to protect her from the advancing horseman. Again, the translation.

Colebrook ignored it all. With one hand extended in a display of peace and one hand on his revolver, he moved steadily towards the couple.

Almighty Voice fired. The eyes of NWMP Sergeant Colin Colebrook widened momentarily, the information he'd been shot registering briefly, and then he fell from the saddle, a bullet lodged in his heart.

The unthinkable had happened: an officer had been murdered. François Dumont reigned in his mount quickly, turned tail and galloped away from his slain comrade. Almighty Voice, too, sprang into action. With a longing glance at his child-bride, he leaped onto Colebrook's horse and headed in the opposite direction.

Yesterday he had been running from a minor misdemeanor, today he was running from a murder. And this was no ordinary murder. The man who lay at his wife's feet was a man of the law. Almighty Voice knew he would pay for this death with his life. He urged the pony onward, leaving the dead man where he lay.

News of the Mountie's death leap-frogged across the prairie from settlement to reserve, to settlers and homesteaders, between police posts and trading camps—the news of the shooting was everywhere.

Colebrook's body was taken to Prince Albert where he was buried with full police honours. That didn't stop speculation on the part of both natives and whites that Colebrook was, in fact, partially to blame for his conduct in such a volatile situation. Negotiations may have prevented bloodshed, but as a poker-faced detachment laid their colleague to rest, they knew no amount of supposition would change the hard, cold facts of the case. Colebrook was dead, and a young Cree brave was responsible for his death. They knew justice would have to be swift and sure.

Despite this resolve, the band of NWMP officers called upon to track the fugitive were met with a wall of silence. No one spoke of Almighty Voice. No one in the native community knew where he was, or if they did, they weren't saying. Even the disgruntled relatives and discarded brides of the handsome warrior chose to keep silent this time. For six months the silence prevailed. A bill posted by the Government of the Dominion of Canada offering a $500 reward for information leading to the arrest of the criminal made no difference. No one would turn in Almighty Voice. No one mentioned his name. Although he lived among his people, stealthily avoiding the law, it was as though he were dead to them when the white men came with their imposing rifles and rapid-fire questions. "Almighty Voice?…" and the words would trail off, as though to indicate the expansive land and the million different possibilities of escape.

Chief Inspector John B. Allan—Broncho Jack Allan to his friends—began to believe Almighty Voice had fled to the United States, or at very least to the land west of Saskatchewan. Every spare man he had, from both the Duck Lake and Batoche detachments, had been scouring the countryside looking for signs of the murderer. An attempt to lure Almighty Voice out of hiding by releasing both his new wife, who was apprehended at the murder site, and his father John Sounding Sky, proved futile. For a full year it was as though the brave had vanished. Frustration for an unavenged murder was mounting in the barracks of the NWMP.

On May 26, 1897, the Mounties got a break. Ironically, it was once again a cow that led to disaster. Two Metis brothers, David and Napoleon Venne, who pastured cattle east of the One Arrow reserve, noticed three natives killing a cow near a sheltering patch of bush. When confronted the natives ran, but not before Napoleon Venne took a good look at their faces. He recognized two of the three men. All were from the One Arrow reserve.

The smallest of the three was a boy called Little Salteaux, or in an English translation of his Cree name, the more prophetic and poignant Going-up-to-the-Sky. One of the other men looked like a former brother-in-law of Almighty Voice, Tupean (other translations of the Cree use the name Dubin or Dubling). Venne admitted he couldn't be quite sure about seeing Almighty Voice, but the largest Indian had his frame and height. The shoulder-length hair, the hawk nose and even the large scar on his cheek matched the wanted poster hung on the barrack walls.

Venne knew he was on to something. He immediately reported his findings to NWMP Corporal William Bowridge, the new commander of the Batoche detachment. The next morning, the two men went back to the dead cow as a starting point to track the Indians. It was a quiet afternoon and only a puff of wind swayed the tops of the trees. Suddenly, Bowridge saw two men dash across his field of vision making for a grove of nearby poplars. The cow killers, whoever they were, were nearby and avoiding police contact. Venne and Bowridge approached the poplar stand cautiously. Before they made any forward progress a shot broke the day's stillness. Venne felt fire in his left shoulder. He'd been hit.

Turning their horses, the two men made for the open plains. A second bullet whizzed through Venne's hat, missing his head by an inch. There were three men in the trees and now there was no doubt about their identity. Almighty Voice had been found.

Bowridge sent for back-ups and the following day, May 28, 1897, the five-acre stand of trees that sheltered Almighty Voice, Tupean and Little Salteaux was surrounded by NWMP and armed civilians. Broncho Jack Allan and his posse of Mounties, including Sergeant Charles Raven, were armed and aiming to see justice done.

What ensued was a ferocious gun battle between the well-concealed Indians and the Mounties intent on flushing their quarry. Sergeant Raven and Constable William Hume were the first to approach the trees. Crouching low and moving slowly, they traversed the woods from north to south, watching for any movement within the trees. It was a brave undertaking and Raven paid dearly for his bravery. He took a slug from Almighty Voice's rifle in his lower body, shattering his hip.

Despite the searing pain, Raven got a few shots away before Almighty Voice and his companions disappeared again into the thick underbrush. Hearing the gunfire, Broncho Jack Allan ordered the rest of his men, including the civilians, to charge the area. Reining his own horse to the south Allan cantered off in hot pursuit. He was the first to be hit. A bullet seared his shoulder and threw him off his mount. Wounded, Allan raised his head and was suddenly looking down the barrel of Almighty Voice's rifle. The native man towered above him, a shadow against the sun. Broncho Jack waited for the shot that would surely finish him off but instead heard the staccato of rapid gunfire. Constable Hume had thrown himself into the fray, firing madly and causing Almighty Voice to take refuge in the woods. Hume hoisted the wounded and now-unconscious Allan onto his horse and made for safety. Raven's men shot round after round into the willows where Almighty Voice had ambushed Allan.

Allan and Raven, were seriously wounded and the outlaws were still in hiding. With officers injured, command went to NWMP Corporal Charles H. Hockin. He quickly sent word to Batoche that medical assistance and more men were needed. He then made an attempt to smoke Almighty Voice out of the poplar stand.

The natives from One Arrow's reserve who had gathered at the scene laughed at the feeble attempt. It was late May and the trees were still green. Told to leave the area by the NWMP, the natives simply moved to the ridge surrounding the poplars to get a better vantage point.

Without food or water, the outlaws would eventually surrender. Their ammunition supplies were dwindling and night was falling. The imminent darkness spooked Corporal Hockin and his next move was a foolish one.

Fearing the fugitives would simply sneak away under the cover of night, Hockin decided to move toward the trees. He suspected the men had dug a pit deep and were waiting to be approached. He was right.

With nine other men, Hockin led the assault on foot, sweeping the bushes in search of Almighty Voice. Shoulder to shoulder the men moved from east to west along the bluff and back again, fingers ready at the trigger watching for the faintest movement in the dense underbrush. Like luckless walkers stumbling on a hornet's nest, Hockin's men found their quarry.

A volley of gunfire shot out of the twilight-tinged willows dropped two of the ten men instantly. Dead were the civilian postmaster of Batoche, Ernest Grundy, and NWMP Constable John Kerr. Hockin was mortally wounded but he lived a few hours before breathing his last as night fell on the battleground. Tupean was likely killed in that exchange of fire, although no one can be sure of his exact time of death.

Now four men were dead. The NWMP were feeling their loss.

Accompanied by NWMP Assistant Commissioner John McIllree and twenty-four Mounties, a posse of men brought in a seven-pound field gun from Prince Albert and a nine-pound gun from Regina. The huge guns were positioned at the foot of the bluff facing the Indian's rifle trench.

From May 29 until mid-morning May 30, 1897, the NWMP bombarded the two surviving Cree from the One Arrow reserve. Amid the roar of the cannon, the sound of small firearms could be heard. Almighty Voice and Little Salteaux defended themselves as best they could in the face of certain death. Overriding the sounds of that last battle—one of the final Indian renegades to wage warfare against the white man's authority—was the piercing wail of Almighty Voice's death chant, a final, parting gift from his mother.

When silence returned to the landscape, the NWMP dared to penetrate the small grove of trees. Shortly after noon on May 30, the bodies of the three defiant outlaws were found. Tupean had been shot in the head. Little Salteaux and

Almighty Voice were atop each other in the rifle pit, both killed by cannon fodder. Evidence of their thirst, the one thing that would have eventually driven them out of hiding, was in the stripped saplings around the trench. They had sucked the trunks of the trees and the tender inside of the bark for moisture.

That afternoon the police carried away their dead—three officers and one civilian—and left One Arrow's people with the bodies of Almighty Voice and his two companions. They were buried amid the very trees that stood as the final testament to a senseless siege that took the life of seven men. Indian legend has it that no birds sang on that burial day.

GUN OF ALMIGHTY VOICE

ERNEST CASHEL IN CUSTODY

11

ERNEST CASHEL: CAUGHT BETWEEN TWO POLICE FORCES

"Take my advice, dear boys, and stay at home, shun novels, bad company and cigarettes. Don't do anything boys you are afraid to let your mother know."

(A LETTER FROM ERNEST CASHEL TO THE REVEREND GEORGE KERBY, FEBRUARY 1, 1904)

Dime novels, tobacco and the company of bad men were what led American drifter and murderer Ernest Cashel from his sweet Kansas home to the bleak gallows of Calgary, North-West Territories, in the winter of 1904. Or at least that's the impression Cashel, a master manipulator, wanted to leave with the world as he ruminated on his criminal career the day before his hanging.

In many ways Cashel took on the persona of the gallant criminals that made drugstore pocket books so popular in his youth. He was unfailingly polite, and many settlers and farming folk in southern Alberta had a difficult time believing that the friendly, charming, talkative lad who entered their lives by the front door left by the back—after stealthily helping himself to their hard-earned possessions.

In fact, so seemingly innocent was the twenty-two-year-old Cashel that many people offered him whatever he needed—food, shelter, a cart or a pony to ride—fully convinced that the polite young man was true to his word and would return their property in due time.

And sweet-talking Cashel was no slouch with a story, either. Before he gained notoriety as a prison escapee and later as a convicted murderer, the young man ingratiated himself to countless people between Ponoka and Calgary, in a part of the country that in 1905 became the province of Alberta. Cashel always had a story at hand as a way to explain why he needed to borrow a horse, or how he came to be wandering the chilly prairie landscape at midnight. He'd say his horse had thrown him, and he'd become disoriented while trying to track it. He once told a rancher he was new in the area looking for land, and his pony had gone lame at a river crossing. Cashel told bold lies, and with his engaging manner and open sincerity, people believed them.

While little is known about the early life of Ernest Cashel, his first appearance in Alberta was in the summer of 1902. He was approximately twenty years of age when he crossed the border to Canada and made his way north to Ponoka, where his mother had secured employment as a bush cook. Some reports say Ernest was a jailbird on the loose from Buffalo, Wyoming, where he was supposed to be serving a one-year sentence for larceny. From the information he gave police officers on his first Canadian arrest, he was born and raised in a small town in Kansas. It's possible both stories are true, but the jailbird-on-the-fly story was backed up with a repeat performance in Cashel's first year in Canada. In October 1902 he was arrested for passing a bad cheque in Calgary.

The forged cheque was the beginning of a downward spiral, and like dominoes in a row, one event led to another, which led to another, all culminating in a noose around a young man's neck.

To put Cashel's escapades in perspective, one must under-stand the policing of the countryside at the beginning of the twentieth century. Larger centres, like the rapidly growing settlement of Calgary, had recently established their own police force. The rest of the land, from the U.S. border north, was under the jurisdiction of the North-West Mounted Police (NWMP) who also had a presence in Calgary. There was some friction between the two authorities, both inter-ested in winning the reputation as the principal enforcer of law and order. Ernest Cashel, in his wild escapades, made fools of both police forces and compelled them to collabo-rate in one of the West's largest manhunts.

That explains why two men—Calgary Police Chief Thomas English and Corporal T.C. Rubbra, NWMP—went to Cashel's workplace, a ranch just outside Ponoka, to arrest him on charges of forgery. Ponoka was NWMP territory, but Police Chief English was intent on taking Cashel back to Calgary himself. This was a way of showing people and the press that no matter how far you fled, you couldn't get away with committing crimes in Calgary.

It was a public relations stunt that went woefully awry.

Travelling back to Calgary on the Calgary & Edmonton Railway that fateful October day, Cashel, handcuffed to English, began to work his mesmerizing charms on the unsuspecting officer. Prisoner and police chief visited ami-ably after leaving the Red Deer station, the chief laughing at Cashel's stories until the prisoner asked if he could use the washroom. Judging the train was moving too fast for an escape, and the small window in the water closet too narrow for a man to squeeze through, English released his charge from the cuffs and allowed Cashel to enter the tiny room alone. It was a deadly mistake.

By the time the conductor was called to break down the door, Cashel was long gone. The window, deemed too small, was gone too—smashed out of its sash, frame and all.

The Calgary police chief immediately needed the help of the NWMP. Judging Cashel had jumped near Penhold, he contacted the detachment in Innisfail some nine miles south of the escape. A two-day search of the area yielded nothing. The police scoured the tracks between Red Deer and Innisfail looking for the spot where Cashel leaped but couldn't pick up his trail.

Meanwhile, almost thirty miles north of Innisfail near Lacombe, Cashel had weaseled his way into the warm farmhouse of settler Amos Driggs. Inventing the name Bert Ellsworth, Cashel told a tale about getting lost and was offered not only a bed and a hot breakfast in the morning, but also the use of the Driggs bay pony. It was as good as kissing the beast goodbye. When the NWMP, who were questioning all the settlers in the area, got around to the Driggs homestead October 17, the slight, soft-spoken stranger had disappeared. Driggs had been duped. He was the first of many.

The escape of Cashel from the hands of the Calgary police department caused an immediate and negative reaction down the chain of command in the NWMP. Almost a month after the train jump, and more than three weeks after Amos Driggs reported his horse stolen, the NWMP Commissioner in Regina, Aylerworth Bowen Perry, received an expense claim from Calgary city police requesting they pay for Corporal Rubbra's trip to Ponoka for the initial arrest. Cashel

Constable A. Pennycuick

was still wandering around the countryside because of Calgary police incompetence and NWMP officers had spent long hours and countless resources trying to find him. In Perry's mind, the Calgary police were charging his organization for expenses that would not have occurred had the NWMP handled the Cashel case from the beginning. The forgery artist and now horse thief must be tracked down and brought to justice, and Commissioner Perry knew just the officer to take on the task. He called Constable Alexander Pennycuick, famed for his dogged pursuit and, ultimately, the hanging of Yukon criminal George O'Brien in 1899. In Perry's mind Pennycuick was just the NWMP officer to prove the salt of the force and put the incompetent city police in its place.

Besides the expense claim that so riled the commissioner, another report had crossed his desk. A settler in the Lacombe area, Isaac Rufus Belt, had disappeared from his cabin on the south shore of the Red Deer River. The report said settlers in the area mentioned that a young, dark-haired, slight fellow had been seen with Belt just prior to his disappearance. The implication of foul play, and the possibility that Cashel could be involved, hastened the need to have the scoundrel behind bars.

Constable Pennycuick led an investigation that would eventually finger Cashel as the murderer of the American homesteader Isaac Belt. All the evidence pointed at Cashel: a man using the alias Bert Ellsworth had stayed with Belt just before the homesteader's disappearance. Belt was last seen on October 27 by his nephew Harry Thomas, twelve days after Cashel leaped to freedom from the passenger train. Young Harry said that he had seen his uncle in the company of a man answering the description of Ernest Cashel.

By early November Belt's relatives, the Thomases, were really worried. Belt had recently built a shack two miles upstream from their homestead across the Red Deer River. He was interested in purchasing the parcel of land but wanted to "camp" on it over winter. Isaac Belt (in some accounts referred to as Rufus Belt) was a cautious man and wanted to see the land in all seasons before he invested in central Alberta property and brought his wife up from Iowa.

The Thomases finally reported him missing November 17. His horse, saddle, a change of clothes—in fact, Belt's best suit—had disappeared along with almost $100 in cash. A fifty dollar American note, relatively rare in those days, was among the missing money. Pennycuick began to suspect that Cashel had murdered Belt, but without a body it was impossible to say what had happened to the settler.

ISAAC BELT'S SHACK

Meanwhile, Cashel was still on the lam. He had headed into Lacombe with Belt's horse and saddle, which had the initials I.R.B. scratched into the leather, and traded them for a horse and cart. From Lacombe he went south to the Sarcee reserve just west of Calgary. A native man named John Isbester reported to police that from November 15 and December 15 he had sheltered a man calling himself Nick Carter. Shortly before Christmas 1902, under the alias of famed American author Nick Carter who wrote Wild-West stories, Cashel moved in with native woman Bella Mitchell. The two took up residence on the reserve but their domestic bliss was short lived.

While the NWMP had been scouring the countryside trying to track Cashel he had been living under their noses. In fact, between November 15 and the time Cashel was apprehended January 24, 1903, the Calgary city police had been to the reserve three times. While they were never able to find Cashel, their uniformed presence was enough to scare him. After intense interrogation by the police, mistress Bella admitted Cashel had fled her house January 11.

Soon after, Cashel approached rancher Glen Healy. It seemed Cashel's horse had wandered off, and he needed to "borrow" another in order to find it. Cashel headed into the Kananaskis hills trying to further elude the law.

After six days, when Healy's horse was still not returned, he contacted the police. Word spread to ranchers and settlers near Kananaskis to be on the lookout for fugitive Ernest Cashel. When a diamond ring was reported pinched from the area, the search shifted to the town of Anthracite near Banff.

On January 24, 1903, Cashel was arrested entering a boarding house. The diamond ring had long been pawned, but he had in his possession Isaac Belt's fifty dollar note and was wearing the same brown corduroy pants that were part of the missing pioneer's best suit.

On hearing of the arrest, Pennycuick rubbed his hands together in glee. The evidence on Cashel solidified his investigation and made him more convinced that Cashel had murdered Belt and disposed of his body, likely in the Red Deer River. Police needed only to wait for the ice to melt in order to start dredging the river.

When arrested, Cashel was charged with horse theft, the theft of the diamond ring, forgery and escaping lawful custody. He was found guilty and received a three-year sentence in the Stony Mountain Penitentiary in Manitoba. It would keep him behind bars until Pennycuick could get the evidence he needed to make a murder charge stick. It seems Ernest Cashel's luck had run out.

On July 20, 1903, settler John Watson went hunting for stray cattle some thirty miles downstream from Belt's camp. He saw the lower back and buttocks of a human body floating in the sluggish river and knew instantly he was looking at the remains of Isaac Belt. Despite combing 400 miles along the banks of the Red Deer River so far that summer, NWMP had not found a body. Watson notified them immediately and together with a coroner and a few of Belt's relatives, they examined the badly decomposed body.

A .44 calibre bullet was found lodged in the dead man's chest, the same type of bullet that Cashel was carrying in his revolver at the time of his arrest. For Pennycuick it looked like an open-and-shut case. He was anxious to lay a murder charge against Cashel.

What followed was a celebrated nine-day murder trial in Calgary—the King versus Ernest Cashel—presided over by Supreme Court Chief Justice Arthur Sifton. The trial, two years before Alberta officially became a province, sparked the imagination of the people in part because of the colourful style of Cashel's defence lawyer, the famed Paddy Nolan. He tried to make Cashel out as a misguided youth. The young man may have passed a few bad cheques and, granted, he did indeed steal a couple of horses, but he would never, never consider cold-blooded murder. Nolan tried his best to paint a pretty picture of the man who maintained his innocence, but the evidence was against them. His defence crashed to the ground on October 25 when Judge Sifton pronounced the sentence. Ernest Cashel was to be hanged in Calgary on December 15, 1903, for the murder of Isaac Rufus Belt.

What followed is the stuff of Nick Carter's dime-store westerns. Ernest Cashel began to receive visits from his older brother John, reportedly up from Wyoming to bid baby brother good-bye. Reverend George Kerby of the Central Methodist Church in Calgary was attending to the doomed man's spiritual needs. During an impromptu bible study with the minister, John Cashel managed to smuggle two revolvers into the jail and slip them to his brother. The Mounties who were assigned to watch over Cashel couldn't have imagined what was to come next.

On December 11, 1903, while the minister was being let out of Cashel's cell, and while a guard was searching it between shifts, a heavily armed Ernest Cashel held three guards at gunpoint until he had secured keys, then locked the guard in a cell and broken out of Calgary Police barracks.

It was the escape of the century, and the press leaped on the incompetence of the NWMP. In a little over a year, Cashel had escaped from both the Calgary City Police and the NWMP. Police Superintendent Saunders wired Commissioner Perry in Regina with the following brief message:

"Cashel escaped by holding up day guards with two revolvers, how obtained unknown, at the time the provost was searching his cell before handing over to night guard. He took revolvers and locked the guards in the cell, obtained keys and unfastened his leg irons. Escape was not discovered until the night guard arrived. We have arrested his brother. It was dark, stormy and snowing hard."

It was a dark and stormy night indeed for the NWMP. The three guards were demoted for their incompetence and one was given a one-year prison term. A $1000 reward was posted and fifty copies of Cashel's photograph were distributed in Calgary and outlying areas. Police quickly notified the CPR to prevent Cashel's escape to the United States. The manhunt started up again. This time Cashel was no young escapee on larceny charges—he was a condemned prisoner, a murderer, armed and dangerous.

The *Calgary Herald* ran story after story of his escape and of the NWMP efforts to re-capture him. Sightings were reported in the press, yet Cashel somehow managed to elude police for six more weeks. Without a doubt, his addiction to cowboy stories and real life crime was part of his undoing.

Reading about himself in the paper, he appeared to love the notoriety and the instant fame, until police asked the *Herald* to stop extensive coverage of the Cashel story.

Ottawa hangman J.R. Radcliffe had been in Calgary since December 14, intending to fulfil his duty with Cashel the following morning. With no neck to place his noose over, Radcliffe was in a state of limbo. How long should he wait in Calgary?

His answer came in the form of a letter, written on Calgary Dominion Hotel stationery from Cashel himself. It was addressed to the Reverend Letch, a Baptist minister: "How are you making it M. Police. I am in good health and spirits for the future life which I am undoubtedly going to have spite the hard work of the M. Policemen. If you do get me it won't be alive. Just tell Mr. Radcliffe he mite [sic] as well go back to Ottawa Ont. And take scaffold with him."

The letter was signed "Mysterious Man" and had a postscript saying he (Cashel) was going to stay in Calgary for "some time yet." It gave police the lead they needed. Cashel was not travelling but instead was holed up somewhere.

A report came in January 21, 1904, from a settler near Shepard, a town just southeast of Calgary. Cashel had held Shepard and his wife hostage while pillaging their house for food and drink. The man said Cashel's clothes were covered in chaff, an indication to police that he was probably sleeping in a haystack somewhere.

At eight in the morning, Sunday, January 24, an entourage of NWMP and a troop of the Canadian Mounted Rifles—thirty-three riders and six men in wagons—rode out from Calgary in search of Cashel. Their orders were to search every house, barn, chicken coop and haystack in the assigned radius. At a ranch belonging to a man named Pittman they found the haystack the fugitive had been sleeping in but no sign of the man himself. A small shack on the property revealed a trap-door in its floor and as an officer descended to check out the cellar, a shot rang out. Cashel was found, fighting mad.

The police decided the best way to bring Cashel back alive was to smoke him out of the shack. Smelling the smoke and realizing his game was up, Cashel eventually surrendered to the NWMP, first securing a promise that he could see his brother John.

On Monday, January 25 the Cashel brothers were brought to court, manacled and bound in iron. John was sentenced to a year in prison in Regina and Ernest was given a week-long reprieve, time enough for the hangman Radcliffe to get out again to Calgary.

There was no question about Cashel's guilt as he approached the gallows on February 2, 1904. At 7:50 a.m., ten minutes before he was scheduled to be hanged, Cashel admitted to the killing of Isaac Rufus Belt. Half an hour later, just the way it ended in the penny novels he was so fond of, twenty-two-year-old Ernest Cashel was dead, his neck broken from the sudden ten-foot drop.

BILLY MINER, THE GENTLEMAN BANDIT

12

BILLY MINER:
A HIGHWAYMAN UNTIL
THE END

At Billy's British Columbia trial, one person responded to a Vancouver reporter's question about public sympathy for Miner this way: "Oh, Bill Miner's not so bad. He only robs the CPR once every two years but the CPR robs us all every day."

When the Gray Fox robbed you, you were well and truly robbed. And maybe a little bit in love.

According to all accounts Billy Miner, also known as the Gray Fox, was Canada's first train robber. A self-proclaimed pacifist, Miner was as polite and as charming as they come.

"Mighty pretty dress you have on, miss. Pardon me while I take all your husband's worldly goods." Add a Kentucky twang, some hang-dog eyes, a handle-bar moustache and you'll have a picture poster of the Most Wanted Man in New Mexico, Georgia, Colorado, Illinois, Michigan, Oregon and Washington, and in British Columbia's Fraser Valley.

Miner, whose dubious career spanned the end of the nineteenth century and the beginning of the twentieth, has gained folklore status as the Gentleman Train Robber. No shoot-'em-up, pistol packin' rogue, this highwayman. But it wasn't just his impeccable manners that brought him legendary acclaim. Billy Miner was the first man to rob the Canadian Pacific Railway, and in the eyes of the farmers, ranchers and miners who lived from the prairies to the Pacific Ocean, that was a noble thing to do.

At Billy's British Columbia trial, one person responded to a Vancouver reporter's question about public sympathy for Miner this way: "Oh, Bill Miner's not so bad. He only robs the CPR once every two years but the CPR robs us all every day."

The CPR's last spike had been pounded into the ground amid great fanfare on November 7, 1885, in Eagle Pass, deep in the mountains of British Columbia. By then, the railway company that had been instrumental in bringing B.C. into Confederation in 1871 was generally perceived in the West as a land-grabbing, money-grubbing institution that only served the interests of an elite group of easterners. Thousands of railway-hating folks in the West protested the grain rates, the land give-aways and the intrusion of the CPR into their lives. Billy Miner tackled the big boys when he sidled up to the CPR with his gun and his grin, and his exploits induced awe and admiration in rural communities in the B.C. Interior and elsewhere across the West.

Canadians try to claim him as a native son, but Miner was actually an American. He was born in Bowling Green, Kentucky around 1843, a son of the genteel South, where magnolia blossoms and mint juleps go hand-in-hand and good breeding means manners as well as thoroughbred racing.

The son of a schoolteacher mother and a mining father, Billy received a cursory public education before running away to become a cowboy. He arrived in San Diego at the height of the Apache-U.S. Army war and saw it as a money-making opportunity. Unafraid to ride through hostile native territories, Miner became a messenger for Brigadier General George Wright, delivering mail to points east of California. Because his hide was on the line, his price was high; twenty-five dollars per letter accumulated quickly, and before long Billy became a big spender. To maintain the lifestyle he had quickly become accustomed to, Billy contemplated a visit to the wrong side of the law.

Young Miner decided fast money could be had ambushing slow-moving stagecoaches laden with pay packets and post or passengers flush with gold watches and silver coins. The quick-in-the saddle Miner robbed his first coach, the Senora, in California. He must have considered the haul, $200, easy money, because Miner continued his antics until nabbed by U.S. marshals who tracked the highwayman down and captured him on April 3, 1866. Miner was convicted on two charges of stagecoach robbery. The penalty was tough: San Quentin prison, one of the dingiest holes in the State of California, became Billy Miner's home for four years. Little did he know that he'd see the inside of San Quentin more than once in his career.

Despite its prime location just north of San Francisco, San Quentin in the mid-nineteenth century was dismal. When Miner was released in July 1870, he had endured torture, isolation, starvation, filthy conditions and beatings by guards and hardened criminals. He wasn't the same happy-go-lucky kid who entered San Quentin and he wasn't long for freedom. Within a year of his release he was robbing stagecoaches in Calaveros County, California and, as fate would have it, back to the black hole of San Quentin maximum in 1871. This time, however, Miner was given a twelve-year sentence for a robbery in San Andreas among others.

He served two years before scaling the walls in his first daring prison break. Despite being captured and thrown into solitary confinement within hours, the taste of stolen freedom must have whetted his appetite for escape, for the Gray Fox was to escape prison five times in a lifetime revolving around notorious robberies and horrific punishments.

After serving nine long years, Miner was finally released from San Quentin on July 14, 1880. In need of quick cash, the Gray Fox quickly resumed his old profession, hitching up with bandit-adventurer Billy Leroy—also known as Arthur Pond—to work the Colorado country. Miner also changed his identity. Working under the alias of William A. Morgan, he and Pond relieved the Del Norte stage of a cool $3600 in gold coin and dust. Before the stagecoach moved on, Miner, his saddlebags crammed with stolen goods, wished the driver a safe journey, knowing the treacherous country the Del Norte had to travel to reach its Salt Lake City destination. The stagecoach may be have been empty of its gold, but ever-gentlemanly Miner didn't want to see needless lives lost owing to careless driving.

Miner must have aspired to a gentleman's lifestyle because he adopted it easily. A change of name, a new city and a packet of stolen cash were the only things needed to establish himself with the best of upper-crust society. Although Leroy had been captured and hanged from a cottonwood tree as a warning to other bandits, Miner escaped custody and by the late summer of 1880 was comfortably ensconced in Onondaga, Michigan, hosting parties, courting women and living a life of genteel respectability, financed of course by his dubious "inheritances." He was known now as William Anderson, a kindly gentleman who knew how to treat a gal properly and who cut a fine figure on the dance floor.

It couldn't last. Miner excused himself from Michigan society and headed back to Colorado to exercise his chosen career, but not, according to some reports, before the entire citizenry of Onondaga came out to his farewell bash. He was charming and could draw an impressive crowd. Even as a robber, Miner was unfailingly apologetic about having to upset the stagecoach passengers. His signature manners eventually became his undoing. Authorities in the West got wind of the Gentleman Bandit and his accomplices, and a Colorado posse was formed in August 1881 to track and capture the Gray Fox and his rag-tag team of ne'er-do-wells.

Success was on the side of the law but not completely. Miner managed to hold up stagecoaches in Arizona and California before being caught by U.S. marshals and shipped back to his old stomping grounds. He was admitted to San Quentin for a third time in December 1881. This time, after a failed attempt to escape, Miner served twenty of his twenty-five years in the pen. By the time he was released in 1901, Miner's livelihood was in jeopardy. Technological advances had ushered in the new century and stagecoaches had been replaced by trains. Labelled a troublemaker by authorities, Miner would have to watch his next move.

But it wasn't such a difficult transition for the shaggy, gray-haired criminal with the immaculate moustache. Afterall, a train was no more than a strung-together stagecoach; more gold, less people to deal with, and in the mountainous terrain of the Northwest, the slow-moving wooden trains labouring up hills were little challenge to a gang of men on fresh mounts waiting in the underbrush.

Travelling north from California, Miner attempted his first train robbery near Portland, Oregon, in September 1903 at a siding called Trout Lake. Miner and his boys botched their first hold up of a Great Northern Railroad train badly. It takes at least three men to rob a train—one to threaten the locomotive crew, one to intimidate the passengers and one to seize the express car where valuables are held. Because of his non-violent tendencies, Miner's task was usually the last. In this Great Northern robbery, one bandit was killed, another wounded, and in typical fashion, Miner escaped without a scratch.

He drifted north to Washington State and eventually found his way across the border to Canada in 1904. What followed was a relatively tranquil period in the life of the Gray Fox. Settling in the Nicola Valley near Kamloops, B.C. Miner re-created himself as a retired rancher who dabbled in land, raised a few cows and toyed with the notion of prospecting. He adopted the alias George Edwards and soon became known as a pleasant grandfatherly type. He was friendly to children, kind to orphans and even gave generous donations to the Church.

When George Edwards left his ranch for business in the first week of September 1904, none of his neighbours knew Billy Miner was back in the saddle. Throwing his lot in with a couple of dubious characters named Shortie Dunn, a Montana outlaw on the run from American lawmen, and Lewis (Scottie) Colquon (also spelled Colquhoan in some accounts), a small-time Ontario crook, the Billy Miner gang was formed anew. The Gray Fox's first Canadian Pacific conquest was planned and executed on Canada's West Coast.

On September 13, 1904, a CPR train, the westbound Transcontinental No. 1, loaded with a gold dust from the Cariboo Gold Mine in Ashcroft, B.C., was heading down the Fraser Canyon for the coast when Billy and the boys boarded the blind baggage car just west of Mission. They crawled over the baggage, mail and express cars and shimmied into the engine room where the chief engineer, Nat Scott, felt a gun in his ribs. Miner ordered him to cut the train behind the express car, pull ahead, then cut the engine off.

From the express car safe, the Gray Fox and his accomplices netted not only the Ashcroft gold dust shipment valued at $4000, but $2000 of gold dust destined for the vault of the Bank of British North America in Victoria, and $914.37 in hard cash. Realizing their booty, the gang scooped up the profits and rode the engine three miles down the track to Whonnock, B.C. A daring leap off the train and a tumble down the steep, rocky banks to the Fraser River, saw the Billy Miner gang escape.

The CPR immediately offered a reward of $5000, or $1500 per outlaw, to anybody who could provide information used to apprehend the bandits. The Dominion government sweetened the pot with more money—$6000—while the province threw in an additional $1500. The rail companies were serious about apprehending the band of thieves, particularly when they knew the public was secretly pleased the CPR was taking a beating.

The second Miner CPR train robbery, on May 8, 1906, was much closer to home, but it turned into a botched business for the Gray Fox and his friends. With Shortie Dunn and Scotty Colquon still in tow, Miner chose to ambush the CPR Transcontinental Express No. 97, fifteen miles east of Kamloops at Duck's Station, bypassing the easy prey of a $35,000 currency shipment on nearby tracks. He was convinced the No. 97 was carrying a shipment of $100,000 subscribed in Canada for the relief of the San Francisco earthquake victims. It was a costly error.

Miner ordered the train be uncoupled, and the mail car, two express cars and engine were separated and moved to an isolated part of the tracks. When Dunn and Colquon climbed aboard, the three bandits rifled through the express cars only to find old mail bags. The gang ended up splitting $15.50 netted from the sacks of mail bound for Victoria. Reports from the CPR say the bandits overlooked a bag containing $40,000 cash—the safe in the second express car also had bullion worth the same. Miner was a day late and a dollar short on all counts; not only did he miss the gold and the cash, but the San Francisco shipment had moved the previous day.

Despite the general ill-will towards the CPR, people in the area were shocked that common bandits could interfere with the stability and almost sacred nature of the government-subsidized rail transportation system. With the cash reward of almost $15,000, a huge manhunt was mounted to bring the Gentleman Bandit and his gang to justice. They were wanted dead or alive.

The 1906 search for Billy Miner included not only common men hungry for the reward, but also hastily commissioned special constables, cowboys, American detectives, railway police, provincial officers and the Royal North-West Mounted Police. Billy Miner had no hope of going back to the Nicola Valley as George Edwards. His face was plastered on every post, beam and tree between Vancouver and Spokane. The Gray Fox was cornered.

The Gentleman Bandit and his gang were discovered near Douglas Lake in the Nicola Valley by Provincial Constable William Fernie. Even though the trio had a fairly credible story about prospecting, something in the leader's demeanour made Fernie suspicious. He reported his conversation with the "older gentleman" to the Royal North-West Mounted Police, who decided to check out the situation for themselves.

MINER'S ARRIVAL AT KAMLOOP'S JAIL

Wasting little time, a party of Mounted Police made their way to Miner's camp. Miner, Dunn and Colquon were squirreling down a campfire meal, confident they had outwitted the law once again, when they were confronted by the authorities. When questioned about the recent CPR hold up, Miner and his gang denied having any part in it. The Mounties weren't convinced. The bluff ended when sudden cheek-to-cheek contact with the Mounties proved too much pressure for Dunn, who pulled his pistol on the posse and made a break for the bush. A round of gunfire caught him in the leg, and Miner and Colquon, realizing the game was up, surrendered themselves without protest. The three desperadoes were taken to nearby Kamloops to stand trial on charges of armed train robbery.

Miner, still claiming to be gentleman rancher George Edwards, carried his new persona through two trials; the first resulting in a hung jury and the second resulting in a quick guilty verdict. Life sentences were doled out to Dunn and Miner, and Colquon received a twenty-five-year sentence. Despite a positive identification from the former San Quentin warden and all the evidence pointing to his past, the sixty-four-year-old gray-haired prospector with the handlebar moustache refused to admit he was infamous stagecoach and train robber Billy Miner. Maybe it was modesty or the notion that bragging was bad manners. Whichever, Miner was sent to B.C.'s New Westminster Provincial Jail protesting his innocence.

CAPTURED: MINER, DUNN & COLQUON

After thirty-four years in San Quentin prison, enduring the New Westminster prison system must have seemed like child's play to the Gray Fox. But a prison is still a prison and Miner continued to scheme his escape. In typical style, he befriended and won the trust of the deputy warden's daughter, who hoped to win his soul for Jesus though evangelical teaching and prayer. Alas, Miner had more worldly aspirations on his mind. After requesting and having been granted permission to work in the prison brickyard, Miner found what was probably the only place in the jail yard where he could not be observed from guard towers. On August 8, 1907, with the cunning of a fox and the help of three young convicts, the Gentleman Bandit dug his way under the fence and vanished over the walls of the prison. A little over a year after receiving his life sentence, the Gray Fox was on the loose again.

Rumour has long circulated that Miner had help springing himself from the New Westminster Provincial Jail. Whether he bribed prison officials or simply charmed his way to freedom is still debated, but one thing is certain: by nightfall of his escape the Gray Fox was headed across the border into the States. Many people in British Columbia were sorry to see him go. His folk-hero status with respect to robbing the CPR, his well-mannered heists and his uncanny ability to escape the bonds of jail had reached cult proportion. The citizens of the Nicola Valley publicly declared they would harbour their friend George Edwards in their homes whether he was the much-maligned American bandit or not.

Miner must have had a homing instinct. It was back in the American South, four years later, that he was once again arrested for a train robbery in Georgia.

The Gentleman Bandit couldn't be kept behind bars. He escaped from the Milledgeville State Prison in Georgia on October 18, 1911 but was recaptured and died on the inside on September 2, 1913, at the age of seventy-one.

Some say he'd tip his hat and wink as often as he'd brandish a gun. But charms aside, Billy Miner, the last of the old-fashioned highwaymen, spent thirty-six of his seventy-one years in prison plotting his escape and how he'd pull off his next great train robbery—politely.

MOSES PAUL

13

PAUL SPINTLUM AND MOSES PAUL: TURNED IN BY THEIR OWN PEOPLE

The chiefs of the First Nations must have felt some shame in the betrayal of their kin, for they collectively refused both the $3000 reward money and the silver medals the government had struck to honour them.

Three men, a bottle of hooch, and a hot day don't necessarily add up to murder, but in the ranching Cariboo country of British Columbia in 1911, the combination was deadly. An argument, a man bludgeoned to death with a rock, and an empty whiskey bottle became the starting point for a massive manhunt that would criss-cross the north country for almost two years, adding a man or two to the death tally as the months dragged on until the total numbered a staggering five dead.

On the Cariboo Wagon Road, twenty-five miles north of Cache Creek near the settlement of Clinton, a settler by the name of Ah Wye had staked out a property and a meagre livelihood near Four Mile Lake. An elderly Chinese immigrant thought to be in his mid-sixties, Ah Wye most likely worked building the Canadian Pacific Railway in his youth, although there are no formal records of his past employment. He retired to Cariboo country to set up a modest woodcutting business. He also kept a large garden, a cow and a few chickens, and his cabin eventually became a stopping point for teamsters and gold miners interested in taking advantage of the summer trade he did in milk, eggs and fresh produce.

Ah Wye was a known teetotaller so when trader William Whyte (in some accounts spelled White) came by his shack on or around July 4 smelling of whiskey, it's not surprising the aged Chinese man sent him packing. But not before two men—twenty-five-year-old Moses Paul, a local Chilcotin from the Canoe Creek reserve, and Charlie Haller, a middle-aged labourer—joined him. According to Wye, the three men left his place together. With Haller on his own horse and Paul and Whyte riding double, the trio headed north to an area aptly called Suicide Valley, apparently to continue drinking and carousing.

Around noon on July 8, a freight teamster named Louis Crosina hurried into the Clinton police headquarters to report a gruesome discovery he'd made on the trail that morning. The body of William Whyte lay off to one side of the path, half-covered by a rotting log. Unlike the three suicides that had occurred in the same area and gave the valley its distasteful name, this was no self-inflicted death—nor was it natural. A blood-stained rock lay near the dead body and its contours matched Whyte's smashed and broken skull. When Constable John McMillan of Clinton came to the death site to check on the corpse, his conclusion was forthright. Whyte had been murdered. A coroner concurred, and after closer examination of the body, judged death to have occurred three days earlier.

In the ensuing investigation, McMillan began to piece together Whyte's movements in the week leading up to his death. The teamster, one of many men who hauled people and goods up the wild trails of northern British Columbia on their quest for gold, had recently been let go from a wagon-driving job near Big Lake, south of Quesnel. He'd been in Clinton to pick up his wages, supposedly coming in on the first stagecoach. The Clinton postmaster informed McMillan that Whyte's pay packet never arrived and by concurrent accounts of a couple of townspeople, Whyte was quite upset and disappointed.

PAUL SPINTLUM

An interview with Ah Wye introduced two new names to the police puzzle—Paul and Haller. McMillan immediately arrested Haller, who was known in town as a troublemaker, and put him in jail on suspicion of murder. McMillan then headed to the reserve to find Moses Paul.

Although known to police, Paul had never caused trouble and it was with some reluctance McMillan approached his cabin. The native seemed reluctant to let McMillan near his cabin and protested loudly when the officer asked if he could search the interior of the house. Claiming he had left the company of Whyte shortly after leaving Wye's place, Paul seemed anxious and, therefore, suspicious. To McMillan it was a sign that there had indeed been some sort a run-in with Whyte. He found the evidence he needed in the house. Wedged between a table and a chink of log in the wall was a pocket watch, later identified as belonging to the dead man. McMillan decided he'd take no chances and, like Haller, Paul was immediately arrested and thrown in Clinton's decrepit jailhouse.

The stolen watch was Paul's downfall. On August 12, 1911, after two arraignments, Haller was let go and Paul charged with Whyte's murder. To McMillan it looked like an open-and-shut case and it probably would have been except for the matter of Paul's daring escape from prison days before his sentencing.

A popular man on the reserve, Moses Paul had a steady stream of visitors while awaiting trial in the log shack with the iron-barred windows that served as his prison cell in Clinton. One of the visitors was his childhood friend and fellow Chilcotin brave, thirty-one-year-old Paul Spintlum. Desperate to win his friend's freedom, Spintlum had his wife bake a salmon, replacing the innards with a metal file. A dressing of wild rice and mushrooms disguised the rasp, and within three days Paul had filed through two of the cell window bars. There was just enough room to squeeze his body through to freedom.

Spintlum also ran. Now an accessory to a murderer, he knew throwing his lot in with Moses Paul was a ticket to life as a fugitive. With a lifetime of hunting and trapping behind them, the men felt they would fare better in the wilds of Cariboo country—the Chilcotin homeland—than any of the people who were bound to pursue them. Spintlum had planned the escape well. Police learned he had rounded up two good horses and purchased a large supply of ammunition for his rifle and general supplies just before the jailbreak.

Armed and ready for whatever the wilderness had in store for them, the two men headed into the bush—but not before making one last stop.

Ah Wye didn't have a chance when he saw who was accompanying Paul Spintlum up the path to his cabin. Paul's face was dark with anger. He saw Ah Wye as a traitor, someone who had betrayed him to the authorities. The elderly Chinese merchant surely must have sensed what was coming. When his body was discovered a week later, his skull was split down the middle. An axe lay nearby, stained with blood. One single, brutal blow had killed Ah Wye and police knew who had done it. The search for the killers was on.

Constable McMillan's first move was to wire the detachment in Ashcroft for assistance. Three constables accompanied Chief Constable Joe Burr to Clinton where the men held a hurried inquest. Ah Wye was pronounced murdered by "person or persons unknown" although all parties knew exactly who their primary suspects were. They just didn't know where they were.

Paul and Spintlum had vanished as quickly as spring snow. Save for a few moccasin footprints around Ah Wye's cabin, the men might as well have melted, so stealthily did they merge with the landscape. McMillan and his colleagues sensed it would be a long, long time before Paul and Spintlum again saw the inside of a prison cell. But, with the call of justice demanding its due, they were determined to track the men down.

Summer turned into autumn and autumn to winter. Despite a large reward for information leading to the arrest of the two men, the police received no tips and no sightings were made. Constable McMillan was sure the fugitives were being given supplies by their families and thus were able to stay well off the beaten trails, avoiding contact with people. The young constable was transferred from Clinton to the coast in early 1912 and, much to his disappointment, McMillan left the area with the murders unresolved.

McMillan's replacement, Constable Alec Kindness, arrived in the spring of 1912, almost a full year after the killings. Besides keeping law and order in the small town enroute to the Cariboo gold fields, his mandate was to close the Paul-Spintlum case and bring the murderous bandits to sure and certain justice. Little did Constable Kindness know, his own life would be sacrificed in the process.

The first sure sighting of Paul and Spintlum came weeks after Kindness's arrival when a homesteader named Charlie Truran stumbled across their camp at a creek crossing around the fifty-mile mark on the Cariboo Trail.

Pretending to look for stray horses, Truran acted as though he didn't recognize the two native men hunkered down around their campfire. He offered them a hefty reward for the return of his mounts, hoping it would be enough cash to make it worth their while to keep him alive. With his heart almost leaping out of his chest, he reeled his horse around, anticipating a bullet to his back. It didn't come. With studied nonchalance, Truran rode slowly in the direction he had come. Once out of sight of the bandits, he spurred his horse towards Clinton.

Constable Kindness responded to Truran's news by immediately mounting a new posse. Now that they had a definite, fixed position on the outlaws, capturing them would just be a matter of a hard ride. Six men, including Constable Forest Loring from Ashcroft, galloped north, picking up rancher Charles Pollard and his son John shortly before they reached Paul's camp. All the men were armed with Winchester rifles and all of them were ready to undertake an ambush on the unsuspecting Indians.

The camp was abandoned by the time they arrived on the afternoon of May 3. Supposing the fugitives had escaped on foot, the posse pursued with renewed vigour. Constable Kindness led the group. As they rounded a bend in the trail, the roar of gunfire sounded. The young officer slumped forward as a splotch of blood flowered on his tunic. The single bullet had lodged in his heart. He was dead in the saddle.

Two more volleys sounded while the posse scrambled for cover. The second officer, Constable Loring, looked down at his arm to see a mass of torn and bloodied flesh. A bullet had almost severed his hand from his arm, yet he still shouldered his rifle and fired into the tangle of trees near the trail head. As quickly as it happened, the attack was over. The natives again seemed to dissolve into the underbrush.

The posse decided to split up. Two men stayed with the slain Constable Kindness and two others rode back to Clinton with the terrible news. A large group of men returned to the ambush site with a cart to bear the body back to town. It was a grim-faced bunch that carried Kindness into the police barracks. Paul and Spintlum had killed a third time and each man and woman who watched the procession carrying the prone police officer shuddered, knowing the murderers were still at large.

ASHCROFT HOTEL WITH OX TEAM IN FRONT

The Provincial Police reacted strongly when they found out one of their own had been felled in the line of duty. Pulling out all stops, B.C. Provincial Police Superintendent Colin Campbell called Chief Constable W.L. Fernie of Kamloops to take over in Clinton and bring with him a team of top-notch Indian trackers. The reward for the men doubled, jumping to $3000 for both. All of Paul's and Spintlum's relatives were arrested as a means of stopping what police perceived as a constant flow of provisions to the fugitive outlaws.

For eight weeks, through one of the wettest summers on record, the trackers followed the movement of Paul and Spintlum, who somehow managed to stay one step ahead of their dogged pursuers. Across thousands of miles the two teams continued their cat-and-mouse game. From Big Bar Lake in the west down through the Fraser Valley Canyon and across the height of land to the Thompson River system, and back to the eastern Fish Lake district, the circular pattern of flight was repeated over and over.

On the eighth week of tracking, the trail suddenly turned cold by the Bonaparte River northeast of Clinton. By the time autumn came around, even the bush-savvy natives were baffled as to where the fugitives were and how they would survive a second winter on the run. The hunt was losing momentum, and the police decided a different tactic was in order.

In November 1912, Thomas Cummiski, the Superintendent of Indian Agencies for British Columbia, decided the assistance of the chiefs of the First Nations in the area must be employed if Paul and Spintlum were to be brought to a court of law. He called together three chiefs from the neighbouring bands of the Chilcotin and Nicola Indians and appealed to their sense of justice. How could they let these men continue in their cold-blooded killing, he asked the chiefs. How could they help men who were so wantonly disobeying the law? There was a veiled threat involved in Cummiski's appeal, too. Underlying his words was the subtle notion that the chiefs could be replaced and new people appointed in the bands, people more to the liking of those who held authority. The chiefs asked for time to discuss the proposal among themselves.

A few weeks after their pow-wow, the chiefs came back to Cummiski with a conditional deal. They would ask the men to give themselves up if both Paul and Spintlum were given proper legal counsel and neither were handcuffed. Cummiski accepted. Believing the chiefs themselves should be honoured for respecting principles of law and order, he had medals forged for each of them with their names and the date engraved on each.

In late December 1912, a year and a half after Whyte's brutal murder, Moses Paul and Paul Spintlum met with Cummiski on the Bonaparte reserve near Ashcroft. There were no other police present and no visible restraints on the men when Cummiski led them to a waiting cart that carried them into Ashcroft. The natives were subdued and, it seemed, somewhat relieved to end their tireless nomadic journey. Both were rail-thin and seemed tired, but a report from an Ashcroft resident said the outlaws each enjoyed a cigar in the Ashcroft Hotel before being loaded on the train destined for the Kamloops prison.

Stuart Henderson, who later went on to defend the famed fugitive Gun-an-noot (see chapter 15) and won his acquittal, served as defence for Paul and Spintlum. He was not so lucky in his plea to the New Westminster jury, who eventually convicted the murderers following a hung jury in Vernon. On December 12, 1913, Moses Paul was hanged in the prison yard in Kamloops. His friend, Paul Spintlum, was given a life sentence, but died of tuberculosis—an infamous enemy of the times—behind prison walls less than a year later.

It was an inglorious end to a lengthy saga. The chiefs of the First Nations must have felt some shame in the betrayal of their kin, for they collectively refused both the $3000 reward money and the silver medals the government had struck to honour them. The medals, inscribed with each chief's name and some words as to why they were awarded, now hang in Victoria's Provincial Archives, a testimony to an uneasy truce between two peoples whose worlds clashed violently and relentlessly at the turn of the century.

Henry Wagner, The Flying Dutchman

14

HENRY WAGNER: THE FLYING DUTCHMAN'S FINAL FLIGHT

For a full year communities along the northeastern shore of Vancouver Island had been plagued with marauders striking from the beaches.

When cold-blooded killer and notorious bandit Henry Wagner of "Butch Cassidy and the Wild Bunch" fame was at last brought to his knees, it was not in a raging gun battle nor in a relentless siege. But that doesn't mean the capture of Wagner wasn't without a remarkable battle in a remarkable, albeit out-of-the-way, place.

Wagner, dubbed the Flying Dutchman in the latter half of his life, was delivered to justice after an intense fist-fight and man-to-man wrestling match that pitted the well-known criminal against a rookie Provincial Police constable in the backwaters of British Columbia.

On March 4, 1913, in a small town on Canada's Vancouver Island, Henry Wagner's final drama was played out, an unlikely stage for a member of Wyoming's Hole in the Wall gang who terrorized the American West for the previous decade. Despite the everyday setting in the final chapter of the Wagner case, a young Canadian police officer would die on duty before the man who ran with the likes of Butch Cassidy and Kid Curry would hang in the gallows.

Union Bay is a ghost town now, and few buildings stand to mark the once-thriving sea port that acted as the shipping hub for the Cumberland coal that was pulled from the rich veins of Vancouver Island. Where once the great trestle-wharf extended out into the harbour for loading coal from rail cars to the hulls of cargo ships, now there are only pylons topped with the rough mud and stick construction of nesting seabirds.

When the mine of Cumberland, five miles inland from Union Bay, dried up, the little town dried up too. Now there is only a slag heap where the coke ovens once burned, and where residences once lined the prosperous street, now only foundations remain. The citizens of Union Bay have either died or moved north to the town of Courtenay and few would remember the huge, clapboard store—the Fraser & Bishop general store—which was the town's shipping, merchandise and supply store and post office. Fraser & Bishop dominated the business district and became the backdrop for the capture of the Flying Dutchman.

For a full year communities along the northeastern shore of Vancouver Island had been plagued with marauders striking from the beaches. Little did they know they were dealing with Henry Wagner and his henchman Bill Julian. Wagner, who after killing a postmaster in Washington State in the spring of 1912, eluded U.S. authorities, stole a boat and started a criminal spree of snatch and flee among the isolated coastal communities on both sides of the Strait of Georgia.

Provincial Police Chief Constable David T. Stevenson was in charge of the region between Port Alberni and Quatsino Sound, one of the Island's most northerly communities. This area encompassed almost 7500 square miles of land with most communities stretched out along the protected eastern shore. And it was on this shore that ports were getting hit by the mysterious night-time bandits. Stores, churches, banks and residences were being broken into and anything that wasn't nailed down was taken. Locals blamed the thievery on "ghost bandits" but with grim smiles they knew the constant pilfering wasn't a laughing matter. Everyone on the east shore was talking about the robberies. Who was doing it? How were they doing it? And why were the police doing nothing about it?

As criticism grew, Chief Constable Stevenson could do nothing but look for a pattern in the robberies. There were marks on the various beaches indicating that the raids were taking place from the water, but Stevenson had little reason to suspect the robbers were professional American criminals, seasoned in hold-ups, train robberies and murder.

FRASER & BISHOP GENERAL STORE

What Stevenson did know was that Union Bay, and particularly the Fraser & Bishop general store, was a likely target for the next heist. Short of officers to guard every coastal town and frustrated by the regularity of the night-time raids, Stevenson decided to focus his energy in one place. Inevitably, he reasoned, the crooks would decide to break into Union Bay's biggest retailer. What they wouldn't expect was a force of two constables ready and waiting to make an arrest.

Because of its busy harbour, Union Bay had one resident Provincial Police officer. That man was Constable John McKenzie, known about town as "Big Mac." Until the spate of lootings, McKenzie's job had been fairly straightforward. The burly, Scottish-born cop broke up drunken brawls between dock workers and sailors and kept the notion of law and order in the forefront of people's minds, particularly when disgruntled miners and their bosses were at loggerheads. Big Mac was a good cop, but like Stevenson, he couldn't be all places at all times. The ghost prowlers had him stumped.

Without consulting Big Mac, Chief Constable Stevenson, stationed in nearby Cumberland, formulated a plan to put an end to the plunder. He had been training two new Provincial Police constables, Harry Westaway from eastern Canada and the affable Scottish-born Gordon Ross, who had recently immigrated to Canada after serving a tour of duty in South Africa. Both men were adventure-seekers, both in the prime of their youth and glowing with confidence and strength. If anyone could crack the case of the seafaring bandits, Stevenson believed these two could. As their first official duty as uniformed Provincial Police officers, the two were to go on an underground assignment specially commissioned by their superior. On March 1, 1913, Ross and Westaway were assigned to full-time watch on the Fraser &

Bishop general store in Union Bay. Stevenson was hoping the ghost bandits would strike at his now-loaded target.

For two nights running the rookie constables held a vigil inside the store. Unbeknownst to the cop on the beat, Constable McKenzie, Ross and Westaway had obtained a key from the community postmaster, the only other Union Bay resident to know of Stevenson's plan. The two men kept a stealthy watch over the merchandise and postal equipment from behind the locked doors of the building.

On March 3, just around twilight as the men started their all-night watch, Chief Constable Stevenson's hunch proved correct.

Westaway noticed a light reflecting in the window of the store. Unarmed except for billy clubs, the police officers entered the building by the separate post office door. They cautiously proceeded into the darkened store listening to the creak of floorboards just beyond. Ross, realizing a robbery was in progress, called into the darkness "this is the police, come out with your hands up."

Before he could finish his sentence, his eyes adjusted to the darkness and he could make out the shapes of two men crouched behind a counter. He saw something else that made him hesitate. One of the men was pointing a revolver. Ross hurled himself downward just as his companion came from behind. A loud crack and Ross felt his tunic wet and warm, drenched with the blood of his colleague, Constable Westaway.

Westaway took the bullet in the chest and collapsed towards Ross and one of the robbers, now struggling together on the floor fighting for control over the weapon.

"There's someone else in here. Get him," called Ross to Westaway. But the young constable was beyond hearing. He was dead from the only bullet fired. As one of the robbers escaped, Ross and the murderer continued to struggle, knocking over hardware and saucepans. A full bail of bolts went skittering across the dark room as the struggle mounted. The man he was wrestling was strong but knowledge of the gun kept Constable Ross fighting for his life. He had to win it.

His antagonist was also battling for his life. The knowledge that he had killed yet another man may have spurred Wagner on. There was no question about muscle or endurance, for he was in fighting trim, the life of an outlaw affording few luxuries. His opponent, however, had the advantage of youth. Wagner finally got the upper hand and closed his fingers around the police officer's throat.

Frantic, Ross jammed his fist into his assailant's mouth only to feel Wagner's teeth bite to the bone, severing two fingers at the knuckle. Blinded with pain Ross felt himself losing the struggle as Wagner hauled back with his gun and pistol-whipped Ross with the blunt end of his weapon. Blow upon blow fell on the officer and, about to give up, Ross found his billy club. Grasping it in his uninjured hand and thrusting up with his last strength, Ross plunged the nightstick into the intruder's belly just as he was about to strike again. The blow winded Wagner and in an instant the roles were reversed.

Covered in blood yet recharged by hope of survival, Ross struck again and again, showering blows to the man's face and neck. Suddenly Wagner went limp. Ross eased up his forceful hammering and relaxed his stance.

It was a premature move. Rearing like a wild beast, Wagner gave a mighty heave, tossing Ross off of himself. The billy club clattered into a display of canned goods, sending them crashing to the ground.

It seemed Wagner, too, had lost his weapon in the struggle, for the men were now engaged in bare-fist fighting. Both refused to surrender, for surrender in such circumstances meant sure and certain death.

With Wagner on top, his hands once again closing on Ross's throat, the two men rolled around the dark store, wrestling in an arena of broken glass and blood. As he began to lose consciousness, Ross felt his nightstick under his left shoulder. He grabbed for the club once more and pounded Wagner until the man lapsed into unconsciousness. Two, three, four more blows Ross laid to the prone body before he realized victory was his. Handcuffing the bruised and bleeding man, Ross turned towards his wounded colleague, about to speak, only to discover with horror Westaway dead and already growing cold on the floor.

Weak with the loss of blood and horrified by the sight of his comrade's empty eyes, the fire of the fight left Ross. With his energy nearly spent, he crawled along the floor toward the picture windows at the front of the store. With his last ounce of strength, Ross threw his billy club through the glass, praying it would attract the attention of some passer-by.

Constable McKenzie, patrolling the northern end of Main Street, had heard the gunshot a few minutes earlier but, because it was muffled inside the building, was having a difficult time identifying where the gunfire had come from. As he approached Fraser & Bishop general store, he heard the sound of crashing glass. Rushing in through the post office entry, McKenzie stumbled across the body of Constable Westaway. The vision that met his eyes once they adjusted to the dark was horrible, indeed. One dead body, and two blood-soaked men greeted him in a ransacked and bloody mess.

The only person conscious was Constable Ross, who quickly identified himself as a fellow police officer. McKenzie, suspicious until Ross was able to produce his Provincial Police badge, did a rapid search of the premises to see if he could locate the second man, after Ross gasped out his incredible story. At the first gunfire, Wagner's accomplice had escaped.

NANAIMO, B.C., 1913

While Ross rested, McKenzie radioed Chief Stevenson in Cumberland. He had a sneaking suspicion the unconscious man, handcuffed and moaning, was no ordinary petty thief. Despite his cut and bruised face, Ross' captive bore a striking resemblance to a "Wanted Dead or Alive" poster McKenzie had seen circulating in Nanaimo.

When he returned to the store Constable McKenzie noticed Wagner was coming around.

"Who's your partner?" he asked, realizing the man was only semi-conscious.

Without thinking, Wagner replied, "Bill Julian."

McKenzie was right! Lying on the floor, subdued by the strength of a single police officer, was the notorious Flying Dutchman, Henry Wagner. McKenzie, jubilant, could barely contain himself.

"You've captured the Flying Dutchman," he exclaimed to Ross. "The most wanted man in the Pacific Northwest is right here. And you're the one who got him."

The young constable winced. His was a bittersweet victory. Constable Westaway's death stole any joy from Ross. Yes, a notorious train robber, highwayman and cattle rustler was finally subdued, but what of his last victim, the lad who had come West hot for adventure only to be mowed down on his first assignment. Ross wanted to see Wagner hanged for the murder of Harry Westaway. Only then would he feel any sense of gratification.

Chief Constable Stevenson, arriving in Union Bay the next morning, confirmed the identity of Wagner. He also spoke with Constable George Hannay who, upon seeing the prisoner, recognized him as one of the men he had seen heading for neighbouring Lasqueti Island by boat earlier in the week. Hannay was commissioned to bring Julian in, and a stakeout of the island resulted in his capture on March 7, 1913. A shack on the island where the outlaws had been hiding divulged much of the loot stolen from the area in the last six months.

With the shadow of the noose hanging over him, Bill Julian was prepared to do whatever it took to save his own neck.

He backed up Ross's account of the night of the murder in the Fraser & Bishop general store, and freely gave the police information on other crimes committed by Wagner.

With Julian acting as the chief witness for the prosecution, Wagner's trial for murder was an open-and-shut case. Once a coroner's jury named Wagner as the slayer of Westaway, the evidence was unrequitable. Henry Wagner, the Flying Dutchman, was sentenced to hang in Nanaimo on August 28, 1913. His betrayer and erstwhile partner, Bill Julian, escaped the gallows and was instead given a five-year sentence for his part in the crime.

The day dawned bright for Wagner's execution. Because the bandit had made several attempts to commit suicide while awaiting his hanging, four guards escorted him to the gallows and up the steps of the scaffold to the spring-loaded trap door. The official executioner for the Dominion of Canada, Arthur Ellis, was at the top of the stairs ready with the noose.

A wild-eyed Wagner stood but a moment on the gallows, and before the first phrase of the Lord's Prayer was uttered by the attendant priest, the Flying Dutchman took his last flight, straight down.

Henry Wagner's hanging on August 28, 1913, was the fastest recorded in Canadian history. From the time the Flying Dutchman stood on the trap until the moment he dropped, a mere forty-seven seconds had passed. It was almost exactly the same amount of time it took for Constable Ross, who had asked to witness the hanging, to finally smile.

Simon gun-an-noot at Hazelton Indian Cemetery

15

GUN-AN-NOOT: THE THIRTEEN-YEAR PURSUIT OF AN ELUSIVE INNOCENT

...he had to run because it was better to be an outlaw in the forest than to trust white man's justice, which after time and time had failed his people.

For thirteen years he ran. For thirteen years he hid. For thirteen years he was tracked and pursued through some of the wildest country on earth. Weary of the hunt, he finally surrendered. After all those years of running, Simon Gun-an-noot was found not guilty of the crime he had been accused of.

All the time he declared his innocence. All the years in exile, while he watched three of his five children die in the wilderness from cold and hunger, exposure and disease, Simon Gun-an-noot claimed he wasn't the person who shot two men in June 1906. But he had been tried and found guilty without benefit of judge, impartial jury or even a court of law. He was condemned by a group of men intent on avenging a cold-blooded murder. In his mind, he had to run because it was bet-

Hazelton, B.C.

ter to be an outlaw in the forest than to trust white man's justice, which after time and time had failed his people.

At a time when the average man brought home under a thousand dollars a year, the British Columbia Provincial Police spent over $100,000 tracking Simon Gun-an-noot. Countless hours of manpower—a full thirteen years —were spent trying to bring a man to justice, a man who, in the end, proved himself innocent, or at the very least, was acquitted of his crime.

Simon Gun-an-noot was legendary for his ability to dodge police, for his ability to survive and persevere in the northern wilderness. He is renowned for his seemingly unending patience. Hunted by the police, it would have been simple for Gun-an-noot to defend himself with a rifle. But he never shot at the men who doggedly tracked him, and he never once felt it was his right to kill in order to defend his hard-earned freedom.

Gun-an-noot was born around 1874, a full-blooded Kispiox Indian and member of the Wolf Clan, a tribe that hunted and trapped the Babine region between the Skeena and Stikine Rivers in northwestern B.C. Theirs was rugged country, rich in furs and men seeking fortunes in trapping or prospecting for gold in the heavily wooded, mountainous terrain. Simon Gun-an-noot was raised in a small native settlement five miles north of Hazelton, the supply centre for trappers and adventurers looking for quick-get-rich schemes. With two hundred settlers, a busy Hudson's Bay store and a small police detachment, it was the closest thing to civilization.

Gun-an-noot, whose name translates to Young Bear who Runs up Trees, was converted to Christianity as a young teenager and lived a relatively quiet life on the Haguilite (or Hagwilget) reserve near Hazelton. Known mostly for his manners—"well behaved...for an Indian," according to Hazelton Police Constable James Kirby—and for his strength and endurance in the bush, Gun-an-noot, at thirty-two, stood over six feet and weighed at least 200 pounds. He was a strong man, but mild-mannered and devoted to his family. He ran a small store on the outskirts of the reserve close to the cabin he shared with his wife Sarah, and first child, a daughter. There they kept a few cows, some horses and a large team of dogs for winter trapping runs up the Skeena River.

Gun-an-noot's peaceful life was forever changed the evening of June 6, 1906, when he stopped at a newly licenced road-house at Two Mile Creek to celebrate a good day's trading. Flush with money, he decided to buy his friends, including his brother-in-law Peter Hi-ma-dan, drinks at the new bush-bar owned and operated by entrepreneur James Cameron. One drink led to two and two to three. While all testimony indicates Gun-an-noot was not much of a drinker, certain people frequenting the public house that night more than made up for his slow imbibing. One man who pounded back the pints of ale on Gun-an-noot's tab was Alex McIntosh, the son of a Hudson's Bay Company trader. McIntosh, who had just been released from jail for selling alcohol illegally, had a reputation for being mean, and meaner still when under the influence of drink. That night McIntosh was out to get drunk and the fact that the big, slow-spoken Gun-an-noot was paying the bill was definitely a bonus.

Because of the intense drinking, testimony as to what exactly happened that night is unreliable. Pieced together from blurry and vague testimony, it seems that some time after midnight Gun-an-noot and McIntosh engaged in a verbal, then physical, fight. Witnesses collaborate that McIntosh started the fight by insulting Gun-an-noot's wife. Blows were exchanged and both men left the bar, angry and disheveled, at approximately 4 a.m., June 7. Some say Gun-an-noot threatened to "get even" with McIntosh.

Regardless of unconfirmed details, Constable James Kirby was given the unsavoury job of examining the still-warm corpse of Alex McIntosh the next morning. The surly packer had been shot from his horse some time after leaving the public house and before reaching town two miles from Hazelton. The bullet in his chest passed cleanly from his lower spine through his heart and to his collar bone. From the bullet's course, Kirby and the coroner concluded that the killer must have been crouched by the trail waiting for the passing McIntosh. Besides kneeling in wait for his prey, the killer would have been an excellent shot, for hoof prints on the trails showed McIntosh had been galloping at full speed when he was gunned down.

As the men gathered evidence at the murder scene and packed up McIntosh's body, a settler arrived with more bad news.

Another body had been discovered on the same trail. The second body was quickly identified as rancher Max LeClair. He had died in the exact same manner as McIntosh; a bullet from behind had punctured his heart and dropped him instantly from the saddle.

Two bodies, an expert marksman on the loose and, according to the grapevine, an angry Indian with a motive. All the signs pointed at Gun-an-noot. Constable Kirby quickly convened the crowd from Two Mile Creek for an official inquiry aimed at confirming his suspicions. The men, some still intoxicated, complied with Kirby's investigation in whatever way they could. Testimony was vague, details sketchy. Yes, Gun-an-noot and McIntosh had argued. Yes, the Indian was known to be a good shot. No, no one had seen him since he left the bar the morning of the murder. Conclusion? Gun-an-noot must have decided to murder McIntosh. Motive? McIntosh had insulted Gun-an-noot's wife. Verdict? Guilty.

The impromptu jury, presided over by Kirby, struggled to make some connection between Gun-an-noot and Max LeClair. Unable to find any evidence linking the two men, they concluded that Gun-an-noot's brother-in-law, Peter Hi-ma-dan must be responsible for that death. Clutching two warrants for arrest on charges of murder, five special constables, sworn in after consultation with Provincial Police Superintendent F.S. Hussey, cantered out to Gun-an-noot's ranch. An uneasy justice clouded their minds.

Only Sarah was in the cabin when the posse arrived, and she had nothing to say to the group of angry and armed men. A look around the property revealed a shocking discovery. Four of the five horses belonging to the family had been shot. The men concluded the killing must have been to prevent them from chasing Gun-an-noot and his brother-in-law should a large posse decide to follow. For some reason the lawmen chose to ignore the fact that several of McIntosh's brothers were reported near the reserve that morning and that the dead horses were likely a revenge killing by the family of Alex McIntosh.

The posse proceeded to the home of Peter Hi-ma-dan only to discover he, too, was suspiciously absent. Constable Kirby immediately wrote out a warrant for the arrest of Gun-an-noot's father, Nah-Gun, who was taken into custody at the Hazelton jail house.

That evening, knowing he must, the sly older native man escaped. Nah-Gun had seen enough of white man's justice to know his son was not safe. But he also knew, without his family, Gun-an-noot would not stay away. Silently, under the cover of darkness, the kin of Gun-an-noot and Hi-ma-dan slipped into the woods to join the fugitives.

Gun-an-noot's mother, father, wife and daughter, along with Hi-ma-dan's wife, comprised the small band of people who left their homes and headed to the land north of Hazelton where Gun-an-noot had trapped in previous winters. Near the headwaters of the Nass River he had a large cache of supplies—ammunition, traps, an axe and three canoes—which would outfit his family and keep them in food over winter.

Meanwhile in Hazelton, pressure mounted to capture the outlaw band. A $1000 reward was posted and approved by Provincial Police in Victoria who also authorized Constable Kirby to swear in and arm six more special constables to man the search. The thirteen-year ordeal had begun.

All summer the posse pursued blind leads and cold trails. An Indian agent from Port Simpson on the Coast got wind of Gun-an-noot's family on the Bear Lake trail and outfitted five men to take up the chase. When that expedition returned to

Hazelton with nary a clue, another team was assembled. Under the leadership of Constable Otway Wilkie, a seasoned woodsman, three special constables travelled to Bear Lake in September seeking signs of Gun-an-noot and company.

Continued defiance from the fugitives was trickling down to defiance in every-day community life. The natives of Babine Lake were engaged in a bitter dispute with government officials over fishing rights. In November 1906 *The Kamloops Standard* reported: "Because of the non-capture of murderers Simon Gun-an-noot and Peter Hi-ma-dan, the Indians in this district are becoming very cheeky and defying the law." Natives were erecting barriers over certain streams to prevent the government from over-fishing their waters.

Headquarters in Victoria believed that suppressing the unrest had much to do with capturing Gun-an-noot, but they couldn't lay their hands on a man who knew every ridge and valley of the land they searched. Constable Wilkie was determined to succeed. When reports of a Gun-an-noot sighting came from Telegraph Trail high in the northeastern corner of the search area, he took his men on the arduous trek through the mountains. They walked and walked, through blizzards of blinding snow, supplies dwindling and tempers flaring. With no sign of the outlaws, Wilkie and his men headed south to the comforts of Hazelton. In the late autumn of 1906 he wired superintendent Hussey in Victoria: "I am convinced not only from my own observations but from the opinion of old trappers in the country, that it is impossible to continue the hunt at present."

The manhunt for Gun-an-noot was suspended until the following summer when, in August 1907 Wilkie tried again. He hired Sergeant F. Murray of the Vancouver Provincial Police and four special constables, two of whom were ex-NWMP.

Two guides and packers, and Constable John Huggary and renowned bushwhacker Bert Glassey made the entourage complete. The plan was to penetrate the northern district of the great Stikine River, separate into two parties, and check the areas where the fugitives had been sighted. One party would paddle up the Stikine, re-checking the Yukon Telegraph Line cabins on the way. The second group, under Wilkie's leadership, would head north from Hazelton to once again scour the Bear Lake territory.

Gun-an-noot was not to be found. On January 31, 1908, Wilkie's weary men returned to Hazelton with stories of deserting guides, upturned boats, lost provisions, deep snow-fall and freezing temperatures. In the course of their search they had walked some 1000 miles through gruelling winter conditions. Wilkie was growing discouraged and the Victoria constabulary even more so particularly when they received a $500 expense claim from Wilkie to make up for what he deemed "the most difficult task ever undertaken by the British Columbia Police in my memory of thirty years in British Columbia." It had been over two years since the murders and the killers were still at large.

In the bush, the extended family of Gun-an-noot was faring with the help of native allies. Sympathy for Gun-an-noot and his family ran high in the native community. When police questioned different Indian bands about tracking the movements of the exiles, they were met with blank looks and stony silence. They kept Gun-an-noot and his family abreast of police movement, sheltered the fugitives in their villages and even gave authorities false leads and misinformation as to the whereabouts of the family.

In December 1908 the Victoria police decided to send some-one out into the wilds who could match Gun-an-noot's bush skills. They chose a prospector named Frank Watson, primarily for his know-how in the wilderness but also because he claimed to have met and befriended Peter Hi-ma-dan the previous summer. Watson said he knew where Gun-an-noot was camped and that he intended to be the one to bring him back alive. There must have been some truth to Watson's claim because he and his guide, Joe Belleway, caught up with Gun-an-noot almost immediately. On January 9, 1909, disguised as prospectors, the two trackers approached the encampment of a large group of Indians north of Kitsumkalum Lake off a tributary of the Skeena River. Telling the group they were searching for the headwaters of the Nass River, Watson and Belleway were quickly exposed as frauds.

"It's winter," said a younger man, a chosen spokesman for the group. "Not even the white man looks for gold in the winter. We don't believe your story." He stroked his rifle. "Other white men have come this way and they have not been heard of since. We want you to leave this place." The message, although veiled, was clear. Seriously afraid for their lives, Watson and Belleway departed the camp on the third day, heading south, while the natives packed up camp and headed in the direction of the Nass River. When he returned to Victoria, Watson publicly vowed never to hunt natives again. He recommended Superintendent Hussey employ "considerable force" in order to capture the fugitives, considering the numerous allies who seemed ready to risk all in order to preserve the outlaw's freedom.

Hussey was seething. Gun-an-noot and his family were making fools of the entire Provincial Police force. At the cost of over $10,000 Hussey decided to hire several American detectives from the Pinkerton National Detective Agency in Seattle. If the Canadians couldn't seem to do the job, maybe the Americans would fare better. It was a last-ditch attempt to salvage police pride and, like every other plan to root out the fugitives, it failed miserably. With mosquitoes, false starts, inconsistent information and the impenetrable bush, the proud Pinkerton men ended up slinking back to Seattle less than ten weeks after arriving in Canada.

The intervention of World War I in 1914 took the pressure off the B.C. Provincial Police and removed their increasingly frustrating search for Gun-an-noot from the public eye. Constables in Hazelton changed postings, the headquarters moved to Smithers and the story of Gun-an-noot, along with the reward, which by this time had risen to $2300, rapidly became the stuff of legends.

Rumours flew thick and fast. Some said a legal aid fund had been set up by sympathizers who were pooling cash to defend Gun-an-noot at a new trial. Others said he and Peter Hi-ma-dan had split up and were now arch enemies vying for the best hunting preserves in the wooded hinterlands. Over the years police continued to launch occasional search missions but the spirit of the chase and the enthusiasm for capture had been over-taken by the Great War.

In 1916, however, something happened that brought the old crime back to the surface. There was a renewed stir in the community of Hazelton. Peter Hi-ma-dan's wife came back to her people to die. On her deathbed, surrounded by natives who remembered the decade-old crime, she confessed to killing Max LeClair.

In a halting, barely audible voice, she said she had met LeClair as she was on her way to the road house in Two Mile Creek to bring her husband home. LeClair, boozy and bold, tried to assault her.

Frightened by his advances, she pushed him away while pulling a rifle from her scabbard. Without thinking she pulled the trigger. Gun-an-noot arrived on the scene the moment LeClair dropped, and according to the confession, he told the distraught woman to be silent about what had happened and to trust him to take responsibility for LeClair's death. Few felt there was much truth to her confession, but it added an unsuspected twist to the dual murder and renewed police interest in getting to the bottom of the case.

Meanwhile, Gun-an-noot was tired from his years of exile. He was now in his mid-forties. Both his parents had perished in the wilderness, as had three of his five children. With his wife also sick, he began to consider giving up the life of a nomadic outlaw.

In the summer of 1917 Gun-an-noot began a dialogue with long-time Yukon Telegraph contractor George Beirnes that eventually led to his surrender. Over the course of almost two years, the renegade native and the old timer would meet around campfires and talk long into the night. Beirnes continually assured Gun-an-noot that he would be rightly represented in a court of law and even volunteered to find him a lawyer. Still somewhat skeptical, Gun-an-noot finally allowed Beirnes to approach a lawyer with the facts.

Encouraged that Gun-an-noot could have his name cleared, Beirnes approached the hot-headed defence lawyer he had in mind—Victoria criminal lawyer Stuart Henderson. Not only did Henderson have impeccable credentials, he was also known for his aggressive tactics and exaggerated courtroom style. He was just the man for the Gun-an-noot "retrial." And luckily, Henderson agreed to take the case. He was keen on his new client, someone who lived by his wits in the Canadian outback for more than a decade.

On June 24, 1919, after much covert wheeling and dealing—including an exchange of a large sum of money between lawyer and client—Gun-an-noot, accompanied by Henderson and Beirnes, presented himself to a skeptical and gape-mouthed Constable James Kirby. Kirby was amazed that the thirteen-year search was over and that justice would at last gain the upper hand. What Constable Kirby didn't know was, that following Simon Gun-an-noot's trial, the police force would look more foolish than ever.

A new trial was set for October. Without breaking a sweat, Henderson tore apart the crown prosecutor's case. Reminding jurors there were no witnesses to either the McIntosh or LeClair murder, and no murder weapon had been found, Henderson easily persuaded the court that Gun-an-noot had been wrongly accused, forced into exile to preserve himself from the hang-'em-high justice of earlier days. After deliberating for fifteen minutes, the jury came back with a verdict of "not guilty." Gun-an-noot was acquitted and on October 8, 1919, left the New Westminster courthouse a free man.

A few months later, in early 1920, Peter Hi-ma-dan also gave himself up to authorities. He was immediately acquitted at a preliminary hearing hastily convened in Hazelton.

The saga of two Kispiox Indians and the extraordinary price they paid to preserve their freedom, and possibly their lives, had finally come to an end. But the question that will probably go unanswered still remains: If Simon Gun-an-noot didn't kill Alex McIntosh and Max LeClair, then who did? Was a miscarriage of justice avoided or was justice ever served? The truth to this day is lost in the wild hills north of Hazelton, where Simon Gun-an-noot, who died of illness in 1933, is buried overlooking beautiful Bowser Lake.

EMILIO PICARIELLO AND FAMILY

16

FLOWERS FOR FLORENCE LOSANDRO, KILLER OR DUPE?

Florence Losandro was not the first woman hanged in Canada, but her story casts the most doubt on the process of justice.

On May 19, 1923, a flowershop just across the street from the Hudson's Bay store on Jasper Avenue in downtown Edmonton received an order for six white, unblemished lilies to be delivered to the prison in Fort Saskatchewan.

The order was from a Franciscan monk, Father Fidelis Chicoine. Days earlier he had been explaining to twenty-two-year-old Florence Losandro the meaning of the lily; how the flower symbolized hope and resurrection, how lilies were a promise from God of new life. Through teary eyes, the young woman asked the priest if he would buy her some. This was no ordinary request, no young girl crush on the handsome parish priest. There was no coyness in Losandro's appeal for lilies. She had no time for that. Florence Losandro was to be hanged that same week for a crime she may or may not have committed.

By the time she went to the gallows on May 2, 1923, Florence was pale and afraid, yet still convinced there would be a miraculous last-moment reprieve. She could not believe she would be punished for a crime she firmly claimed she didn't do. The flowers had not arrived.

But they did come the afternoon of Losandro's death, and when the lilies came—pure, white, almost translucent blooms of incredible fragility—they were a bleak reminder to the prison guards and jailkeepers of the terrible task they had just completed and the niggling fear that innocence had somehow been destroyed.

Florence Losandro was not the first woman hanged in Canada, but her story casts the most doubt on the process of justice. She did not go to the gallows alone. An hour before her small body was cut from the rope, bootlegger Emilio Picariello had died the same way. Emperor Pic, as Picariello was known in the foothills of southern Alberta, also proclaimed his innocence as the trap door opened and his 200 pound frame dropped to the ground. Each blamed the other, and as no one is certain who fired the awful shot that felled a young police officer, both were executed on a Fort Saskatchewan scaffold.

The story of Losandro can't be told without the interconnected tale of Emilio Picariello, the biggest bootlegger of Crowsnest Pass. But to truly understand Losandro's position in the rum-running and whiskey-trading of the Prohibition years, it is essential to understand her childhood and the narrow constraints of her traditional upbringing.

Born Philomena Contanzo in Cosenza, southern Italy, Florence and her family immigrated to the Crowsnest Pass area of British Columbia when she was nine years old. Her father Vincenzo worked on the Kettle Valley Railway, eventually settling his family in Fernie where he worked in a coalmine. Other Italians came out to the New World at the turn of the twentieth century and, like the Contanzos, settled in small coalmining towns between Fernie and Pincher Creek.

With language and customs in common, the Italian community grew. Despite being scattered across the small towns between towering mountain ranges, they remained closely connected to each other, and conversely, were somewhat isolated from the English-speaking people of the region.

As was the tradition in Italy, Philomena was given in an arranged marriage to a twenty-three-year-old fellow immigrant, Carlo Sanfidele, who lived just a few communities east of the narrow B.C. valley before it opened into the rolling plains of Alberta. It was a loveless marriage from the beginning. Philomena, whose name was immediately changed to the English version, Florence, by her fiancée, was given no choice in her groom. When she married Carlo in October 1915, she was only fourteen years old.

Raised to be subservient to her husband, Florence had little choice in the decisions that would affect her turbulent life. Immediately after marriage, Carlo moved himself and his new bride to Pennsylvania where he was involved in dubious activities, likely Mafia related. Fleeing the States two years later, Carlo and Florence assumed the surname Losandro in an effort to cover their tracks and keep the U.S. lawmen at bay.

Florence was happy to be back in Fernie but many changes had taken place over a relatively short period of time. In the course of four years a very young woman was transformed from a fourteen-year-old child, Philomena Contanzo, to bride and domestic servant of Carlo, to Florence Sanfidele and finally, back in Canada, she had become Flo Losandro, the name she would take to her grave. Still very naive, Florence didn't realize the name change was to protect her husband from organized crime. She was unaware that crime had entered her life in America through her husband's dealings. Canada would prove not that much different, particularly when Carlo hooked up with businessman Emilio Picariello, the emperor of all boot-legged liquor in southern Alberta.

On July 21, 1915, after months of tireless campaigning by the National Women's Christian Temperance Union, the Province of Alberta voted for Prohibition. The *Liquor Act* was poorly worded and almost impossible to police. It wasn't illegal to manufacture liquor in Alberta, nor was it illegal to sell to some-one outside the provincial boundaries. The purpose of the Act was to prohibit the sale of intoxicating liquor within the Province of Alberta. It was legal to consume a limited amount of liquor—a quart of whiskey and two gallons (approximately one case) of beer—within your own quarters, provided the alcohol wasn't secured in Alberta.

Meanwhile, the province of B.C. was wet and trying its best to disregard the temperance movement altogether. So it was almost inevitable that the Crowsnest Pass, where the Italian community had put down roots, would become a bootleggers' highway. And who had set up shop just east of the B.C. border? Emilio Picariello and his sidekick, Florence's husband Carlo Losandro.

Their moneymaking mission was to get B.C. alcohol into the hands of the poor, thirsty Albertans. It was exporting illegal goods, granted, but exporting nonetheless. Picariello, who, prior to prohibition in Alberta and Saskatchewan made his living in Florence's hometown of Fernie selling first pasta, then cigars and finally ice-cream, gave up the life of an honest citizen when he realized the money to be made in illegal liquor trading.

In 1917 the Alberta Provincial Police force was organized, and Picariello purchased an old hotel in Blairmore, Alberta, just across the border but close enough to the B.C. stills. He was determined to get his loads of liquor through to Alberta.

With a fresh new police force on one side, and an entrepreneurial Italian on the other, the teams had been chosen for the bootlegging war. One of the mandates of the newly established Alberta Provincial Police force was to eliminate illicit alcohol smuggling. They needed the help of the B.C. government and on July 1, 1917, British Columbia adopted some measures of prohibition. The new force realized under the current Act, that importing alcohol to Alberta was too easy. The government agreed any shipment over the allotted one quart of spirits or two gallons of beer was illegal.

Less than a year later, however, with the temperance movement lobbying hard, all liquor shipments to the province of Alberta were curtailed. Moonshiners and bootleggers who operated the sixty-five-mile Rocky Mountain pass between the provinces had to go underground. In his new headquarters, the Alberta Hotel, Picariello was ready. So were the Alberta Provincial Police.

Carlo and Flo, meanwhile had been ensconced in the Alberta Hotel, Carlo overseeing the digging of tunnels between the hotel's garage and its basement. When cars were parked in the garage they were hidden from view. No one could see what went in or out of the basement of the hotel. It was a bootlegger's dream.

While Florence waited tables in the hotel dining room and played nursemaid to Picariello's wife Maria and their seven children, the two men gathered a stable of three of the fastest cars on the road, the McLaughlin Sixes (later known as the Whiskey

Sixes), an extremely competent mechanic named McAlpine, and a team of chance-taking drivers. Pic had the cars equipped with large, weighted gas tanks for long hauls and concrete-enforced bumpers to plow through police blocks and keep the vehicles weighted to the road for maneuvering the tight curves of the mountain pass.

A year later in 1919, the state of Montana was declared totally dry. Emperor Pic was laughing. He had the fastest cars on the road, a legitimate front for his bootlegging activities and he began openly defying police by running alcohol from B.C to Alberta and Montana.

By 1919 the economy in the Crowsnest Pass was booming. It wasn't just alcohol that was fetching a pretty penny either. Lumber and coal prices were up. Men had more money for extras. The bootlegging business was doing a roaring trade. Police were getting frustrated with the rum runners and the provincial superintendent sent word to all detachments that it was time to crack down on illegal liquor trade. Like a canary chased by a cat, Emperor Pic knew he'd have to keep just out of reach.

He formulated a plan that involved a decoy, Florence Losandro. She became the pawn of one of the biggest booze smugglers in the country. It was a move that would eventually kill her.

Florence, pensive and pretty, was just the person the Emperor needed to distract the police. Together with Pic's oldest son Stephen, affectionately called Stefano by his parents, the two young people would take an empty car through a checkstop, pretending to be lovers on a picnic. In a designated meeting spot back in the hills, after a pick-up at a moonshiner's still, they would exchange their empty McLaughlin for a loaded McLaughlin.

The plan to bring the alcohol-laden vehicle back through the checkstop without being searched depended on the officer remembering checking the car earlier. Florence, with her slim figure, dark eyes and blushing shy smile, was not easily forgotten. If she engaged the officer in conversation on the way through the check, asking him where she and her lover could be alone, surely she would be waved though on the return journey.

Emperor Pic saw it as the perfect ploy to ensure another full load of alcohol got stashed in the basement of the Alberta Hotel for further distribution in small towns.

Liquor trickled into the hotel from many sources. Some came via rail from British Columbia where selected and well-paid station agents would hold a shipment until the McLaughlin cars could pick it up. But most depended on taking loads in and out with his own drivers. In the bootlegger's mind, a pretty girl was a perfect distraction.

For Florence, the road trips were a much-needed change from working in the hotel and looking after Emilio's children. If her husband Carlo didn't pay her any attention, at least Pic's drivers did. It was part of her job to pretend that she and Emilio's son Stephen were lovers—and she may have wished that were true.

Florence, always doing as she was told, soon became addicted to the life of high-speed chases with the police, and the excitement and attention from men more her own age. She seemed oblivious to the dangers of her new profession. What she didn't realize was that drivers always had her sit in the back seat, ready to show her face out the rear window when pursued by police. Decorum in the 1920s still ran high. They were banking that officers wouldn't shoot at a car carrying a woman.

Florence Losandro was a decoy in more ways than one. Her presence was valuable to the men, not only because of her feminine charms and easy smile, but because she was a human shield preventing them from being shot at. Her husband, ever faithful to his employer, agreed Florence was a valuable asset in the whiskey trade. He let Pic take her on all the rides he needed to ensure the money and the illegal alcohol would continue to flow across the borders and pad his own pocket.

Emperor Pic was a two-sided man, and police were fully aware of his status in the valley as a sort of modern-day Robin Hood. He was an extraordinarily generous person who gave to the needy and donated great sums of money to various causes in the community. In January 1921, the well-known bootlegger was actually elected to the Blairmore Town Council. His newly acquired status in the community did nothing to diminish his alcohol trade, however. Nor did it stop the police from trying to catch him with a load of illegal drink going out of or coming into the basement of the Alberta Hotel.

Now over forty, Emilio was becoming less and less involved in the actual runs and instead allowed his son Stephen to take over the driving of the illegal booty. Occasionally he would go along, however, and it was on one of these rare runs, September 21, 1922, when father and son travelled in convoy, that fate played her ugly hand.

Three McLaughlins were involved in the trip from Fernie across the B.C. border into Alberta. Stephen Picariello drove the first car, fully loaded with liquor; McAlpine the mechanic drove a second car, also loaded; and Emilio drove the third car, carrying no liquor. The plan was to drop the load of liquor at Picariello's hotel in Blairmore.

Constable Stephen Oldacres Lawson was a new police officer stationed in Coleman. He and Sergeant James Ogston
Scott, stationed just a few miles east in Blairmore, had been
recruited scant months earlier specifically for the purpose of
adding new blood and fresh energy to the area in the hopes
they would be instrumental in curtailing the liquor trade.
Because the men hadn't lived in the community long, they
were not taken in by the charms, status and generosity of the
large Italian man who called himself Emperor Pic. To them
he was a bootlegger, plain and simple, a man recklessly disobeying the law.

It was forty-two-year-old Lawson who saw the McLaughlins
idle down Coleman's main street in broad daylight that autumn
afternoon in 1922. He radioed ahead to Constable John Dey at
the Provincial Police detachment in Frank, Alberta, who with
Sergeant Scott, hurried over to Blairmore. Sure enough, by the
time the two officers reached Blairmore's main street, there was
Emilio Picariello lounging against his perfectly polished car outside of his perfectly innocent-looking hotel.

This time, however, the police officers had come armed with a
warrant. They told Emperor Pic they intended to search the
hotel, particularly the basement area where, rumour had it, illegal alcohol was stored. Pic didn't seem to respond to the information that a raid was underway. He simply leaned over and
tooted the horn of his car. It was, of course, a warning to his son
Stephen. Don't approach with the load, the horn blasted, the
police are here already.

Suddenly a second McLaughlin pulled out of a side street
and, screeching its tires, wheeled west in the direction it had
come. The police knew instantly they had interrupted a drop
and the car heading back to the border was still loaded with
booze. It looked like an arrest might be possible at last.

Corporal Dey and Sergeant Scott leaped into their police car at the same time Emilio jumped into his McLaughlin. Both cars tore after the young Picariello, the police to apprehend him, his father to protect him. The Whiskey Sixes were the winners. Emilio's empty vehicle covered the tail of his son's car as it rushed to get across the provincial border. Dey suddenly had an idea.

"They're doubling back through Coleman. We'll get Lawson to stop them on route." The officer rushed to the phone in Blairmore's Green Hill Hotel.

Lawson, receiving the call, knew he didn't have much time to waste. He commandeered the biggest car he could find from local resident William Bell, then hurried down to the main street on foot. Lawson stepped into the middle of the street in the path of the McLaughlin as it sped into town. He raised his hand to stop the car but the McLaughlin didn't even slow. It sped onward, straight towards the constable. It was a deadly game of chicken but Stephen Picariello was not about to turn off course. At the last second, Lawson jumped aside. The McLaughlin swerved and continued down the street.

Instinctively Lawson went for his gun and fired two shots at the retreating car, aiming at the tires. He leaped into Bell's car and ordered him to follow the speeding McLaughlin. Weaving west through the mountainous pass, the deep black waters of Crows Nest Lake on their left, the two cars screamed around corners, Lawson in hot pursuit of the bootlegger's boy.

With the McLaughlin in range, Lawson leaned out the window of Bell's car, pistol in hand. He let out a final shot before he felt his car slowing and saw the Whiskey Six roar ahead.

CONSTABLE STEPHEN OLDACRES LAWSON

"I shot wide. Why the hell are we pulling over?" he asked the driver.

"We've got a flat," said Bell, and sure enough, his car was listing badly to the right, the front driver's side wheel flattened to the rim. Getting out to examine the tire, the two men saw another McLaughlin pull up towards them. It was Emilio Picariello's vehicle.

"You had better bring your son back, because if you don't get him, I will," Lawson said, leaning into the window of the older Italian's car. He was still angry, still flushed from the chase and the adrenaline of danger. Pic simply drove away, his face Bell described as "a mask of anger."

At this point the Emperor was not aware that shots had been exchanged. Nor was he aware that his oldest boy, the beloved first-born who was taking over daddy's bootlegging business, had been hit by Lawson's final bullet. The Crowsnest Pass, long saturated in booze and bravado, was now stained with blood. And revenge was not far off.

Florence was at the Alberta Hotel in Blairmore when Emilio got the news that his son had been hit by the policeman's bullet. What he didn't know was that the bullet had only grazed Stephen's hand, leaving a superficial wound. In Emperor Pic's mind, the worst had happened. His precious boy was dead. McAlpine, the mechanic and driver of the second car, had gone across the border to find information on Stephen.

Frantic with worry, Emilio could only think of revenge. Florence, gathered in the kitchen of the hotel with the rest of the extended family, listened quietly while the men spoke in Italian. She was worried about Stephen, who, over the months of driving, had become her fantasy boyfriend.

Emilio's wife Maria was weeping bitterly. Carlo and some of the other drivers were trying to calm down Emilio who seemed beside himself with rage and sorrow. He paced back and forth muttering between sobs: "He will pay. A bullet for a bullet. My boy! My poor Stefano!"

Carlo tried to comfort his boss, urging him to wait until they got news on the boy's condition, but Pic would not be dissuaded from his plan to get even. His eyes ranged around the room and fell on the hapless Florence, sitting off to one side. Something changed in his eyes. "Get your coat," he said. A decision had been made, and for reasons known only to Emperor Pic, Florence Losandro had been chosen as his accomplice.

Ever compliant, Florence did as was commanded. Her husband remained mute as the two of them ducked into the waiting McLaughlin and headed back up the mountain pass to the town of Coleman to pay a visit to the trigger-happy policeman who dared to fire his pistol at the Emperor's son. Pic placed a small .32 caliber Colt automatic pistol in Florence's hand. He held the other, a .38 caliber revolver. Both guns had been licensed for business protection in April of that year.

"For protection," he murmured as the lights of Coleman came into view around the bend.

Lawson was just preparing to partake in an evening meal when the car pulled up outside the police barracks that also served as a home for his wife and four children. The youngest child called her father to the door when she didn't recognize the people sitting in the big shiny car outside. She remained in the doorway as her father came out to speak to them. According to the child's testimony, one of the people in the car was "a lady with a red tam."

Words were exchanged and the two men engaged in a tussle. Lawson's arms were around Picariello's neck when a shot rang out. Then a second bullet hit the speedometer and smashed through the windshield. Lawson turned towards the barrack for protection. A third shot shattered the cool mountain air. Before the eyes of his horrified daughter, Constable Lawson crumpled to the driveway as the big car gunned its motor and sped away.

Lawson died moments later, as his wife and children rushed to his side. The bullet, a .38 caliber slug, had entered his back below the shoulder blade, severing his aorta. He didn't have a chance.

Word quickly spread that an officer of the Provincial Police had been murdered by a member of the bootlegging business. A detachment of the RCMP descended on the area and scores of Provincial Police were contacted and told to go to the Crowsnest. The force was determined to hunt down the murderers as quickly as possible.

Sergeant Scott was totally shocked at the violence perpetrated on his colleague and, because he had recently had contact with Lawson, he was sure it had to do with the high-speed chase that afternoon. With a fellow constable in tow, Scott staked out the Alberta Hotel in Blairmore. At 3 a.m., September 23, his patience was rewarded when one of Picariello's McLaughlin Sixes came limping in, driven by the operator of Blairmore's taxi stand, Alberto Dorenzo.

"Found it back by a shack near the Cosmopolitan Hotel. Thought I'd best bring it into town," said Dorenzo, hastily abandoning the idling car.

Scott and his colleague descended on the vehicle searching for clues. They didn't have to look far. On the front seat lay a live .32 automatic cartridge. The windshield was shattered and the speedometer was broken. There was no question that this was the murderer's car. And the murderer must be the unaccounted-for Emperor Pic. But police were still baffled by Lawson's daughter's statement that "a lady" had been in the car. Who was the woman in the red hat?

Meanwhile Florence and Emilio had found shelter in a small shack on the outskirts of Blairmore. Both were badly shaken. Picariello was babbling: "Tell them you did it, just you, in self-defence," said Pic to a pale, trembling Florence. "I will be blamed but, because you are a woman, they can't blame you. It was to protect yourself. Women must protect themselves. It is allowed. Listen, you say you did it, and I will go free and with all my money I will find you the best lawyers. Then you will go free too."

Florence Losandro only nodded mutely.

Through the long night of the murder, police in Blairmore had been searching the Alberta Hotel looking for evidence. In Flo's room they found two Dominion boxes containing forty-eight .32 caliber automatic shells. In Emilio's and Maria's room more ammunition was discovered. In the bottom drawer of a dresser were thirty-six shells of two different makes, both fitting the same .38 caliber revolvers. Now the police had the murder weapon, the murder car, and evidence linking the suspects to the weapons—all they needed were the suspects themselves.

At noon later that day, September 23, 1922, Emilio Picariello was arrested near the shack on the outskirts of Blairmore by B.C. Provincial Police Constable Bradner and RCMP Officers Tutin and Clark. Pic surrendered to the police shortly after being surrounded. His first question was about his son Stephen.

"Tell me, please, how is my boy?" said Pic, hands raised.

"He's fine," growled Tutin.

"And the other? Lawson?"

"Dead," came the grim reply.

As he was bundled into a waiting police car, witnesses say Picariello looked genuinely surprised to hear of Lawson's demise. There was no sign of Florence at the cabin. She had left early in the morning and walked, dazed and confused, to the home of a family she knew. She was arrested there three hours later with no struggle. She seemed calm and unaware of the trouble she was in. Wedged between the cushions of the sofa was the gun Pic had started out with, a .38 caliber revolver.

Like an automaton, Florence Losandro made an unprompted confession to the police at the Blairmore barracks saying she had shot Lawson after two shots were fired into the vehicle. "I killed him by accident," she said, without emotion. "There was only one gun in the car."

Her testimony contradicted the evidence police had already found both in the car and on her person, but her confession was sufficient to lay murder charges. Emilio was taken to Lethbridge Jail pending a preliminary hearing October 2. Florence was taken immediately to prison in Calgary. It was decided the two would be tried jointly, but in order to ensure a fair and unbiased jury, the trial would have to be moved to Calgary. Sentiment in the Crowsnest Valley was strongly against them. The Italian community was stoic and silent. The rest of the people could talk of nothing but the murder. On the day of Lawson's funeral, Monday, September 25, public opinion raged against the bootleggers and against the government that had engineered the battle for the bottle. In many minds it was Prohibition that brought death to the region.

One man writing a letter to the editor of the *Lethbridge Daily Herald*, October 1922 said: "This is an awful toll for the *Liquor Act*. I voted for Prohibition but never again will I vote for it in its present form. In the old days we had two regulated saloons and some semblance of law and order. Now we have twenty-one places to get liquor and you all know what we have as the aftermath of this [Lawson] shooting! A dead officer, a widow and fatherless children! The price, in my opinion, is too high. This murder will be the death knell to bootlegging in the Pass."

The trial of Losandro and Picariello versus the King was finally scheduled for November 27 in Calgary's Supreme Court. Attorney General John E. Brownlee acted as crown prosecutor with lawyer McKinley Cameron acting as senior council for the defence. The week-long trial included testimony from Lawson's nine-year-old daughter who had witnessed the entire killing, and the evidence found by police immediately following the murder. While it was still unclear to the courts who had fired the fatal shot, the fact that Losandro and Picariello collaborated in the crime led to the verdict. Both were declared guilty of murder and sentenced to hang in Fort Saskatchewan. The Honourable William Justice Walsh read the sentence to both prisoners: "You will be taken from your place of confinement on February 21, 1923, and on that day you will be hanged by the neck until you are dead. And may God have mercy on your soul." Pic blanched. Flo wavered unsteadily on her feet. Justice was satisfied.

Deep in her heart, Florence Losandro still believed she would not be hanged. McKinley Cameron, asking for an appeal hearing on January 29 in Edmonton, buoyed her hopes. Hadn't the Emperor told her to confess to the crime so she would get off because of her gender?

The appeal was dismissed by the Appellate Division of the Alberta Supreme Court. However, a stay of execution was granted. Flo's new death date was moved up a month. Her lawyer now had until March 21 to have her sentence reduced.

It was in the late winter of 1923 that Florence began to talk in earnest with the priest who routinely visited death row in the bleak prison in Fort Saskatchewan. In trying to reach the desperate girl's soul and win the truth from her, Father Chicoine told her about the lilies and about hope for those who believed in the death and resurrection of Jesus Christ. Maybe feeling Picariello was no longer a Saviour, Florence asked the priest to buy her the lilies should the awful moment come.

Frantically working to save Florence from the gallows and believing her to be wrongly accused, Cameron appealed to the Supreme Court of Canada. Again, a reprieve of one month was granted but the execution day, now May 2, continued to torment Florence. When her last appeal was turned down, she fell into a deep depression.

In a last bid to save the girl from hanging, Cameron approached the Minister of Justice on April 24 and urged clemency for his client. For two decades women condemned to death in Canada had always had their sentences commuted owing to their gender. In Ottawa, far from the girl languishing in the Fort Saskatchewan prison, Sir Lomer Gouin was not moved. He would not go against the highest court of the land. Florence Losandro would pay the price of her cowardly crime.

While Emilio Picariello got his affairs in order, writing lengthy letters to his wife and oldest son Stephen about the business, Florence Losandro waited for him to admit he alone had pulled the trigger.

At 4 a.m. on the morning of May 2, the hangman, the coroner and the officials of the prison gathered to prepare for the unpleasant task ahead of them. It was agreed Emilio Picariello

FLORENCE LOSANDRO

should be hanged first, in the hopes that, on the gallows, he might make a declaration to clear Florence's name. After a large breakfast of bacon and eggs, Emperor Pic was given two ounces of Spiritus Frumenti, the bootlegger's last drink. At 5:15 he was led up the eighteen steps to the top of the scaffold. When asked if he had any last words Pic replied: "You are hanging an innocent man. God help me."

Ten minutes later the body of the bootlegger was cut down and taken away. Florence Losandro, who had also received an ounce of alcohol and a half-gram injection of morphine, was next to be hanged. Quaking, the slight woman paused on the gallows for only a moment. Her last words before the door was sprung were also of her innocence. "I didn't hurt anyone. Ever." And then the spring, the drop and silence.

Whether innocent or not, Florence Losandro first assumed responsibility for Lawson's death thinking that, as a woman, she would have a better chance of escaping the gallows. She was wrong and may have been badly betrayed. According to the priest who laid the lilies on the rough box that contained her body, Florence Losandro's stand was more heroic than it was wise. She paid an awesome price.

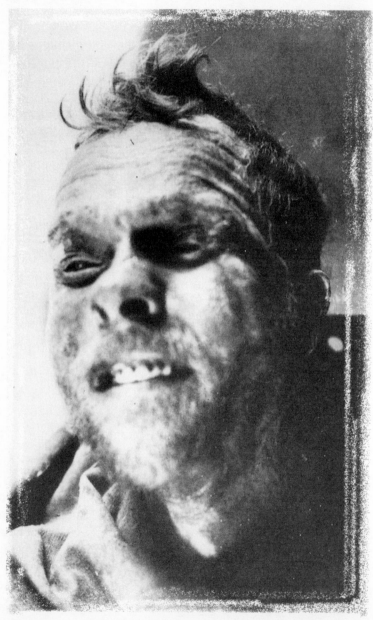

ALBERT JOHNSON IN DEATH

17

THE MADNESS OF ALBERT JOHNSON, RAT RIVER TRAPPER, 1932

…the Arctic Circle War captured the imagination of the Depression-weary residents in southern Canada and in the United States.

The legacy of Albert Johnson is a legacy of cat and mouse, a game of avoidance and elusion that played itself out in the frigid chill of mid-winter 1931–32, high in the Canadian Arctic. The game became deadly serious when police blood stained the pristine snows that cover the rugged landscape along the Yukon-Northwest Territories border. Two men were injured and at least one died during the Royal Canadian Mounted Police's forty-eight-day onslaught against Albert Johnson. The blood-stained snow was a testimony to the courage and determination of the posse of men who tried to bring down the Mad Trapper of Rat River. It was also a reminder of how one crazed madman kept almost a dozen skilled and seasoned police officers and experienced woodsmen at bay and how that drama, dubbed the Arctic Circle War, captured the imagination of the Depression-weary residents in southern Canada and in the United States.

Johnson's tale begins at the beginning of the twentieth century in Sweden, half a world away, where the winters rival those of the Canadian Arctic. Exploration, arctic adventure, the New World, the glory of the North—these are the dreams that propelled a young man from the safety of home across a dark sea to a new life in a new land. In the case of Albert Johnson, it wasn't just a desire for adventure that made him come to the New World—it was anger. Apparently, a falling out with his Swedish girlfriend and the souring of that relationship drove a emotionally battered Johnson to Canada in 1926. He was thirty-two years old. By the time Johnson had worked his way up the St. Lawrence River to Montreal, he was still a deeply bitter man.

Just shy of his thirty-third birthday Johnson met a fellow adventurer, a French Canadian man with a booming voice and even bigger dreams. Together, probably over pints, they discovered how much they had in common. The North was calling them.

In May 1926, Johnson and his partner followed the lengthening days to the North, settling in the region of the Northwest Territories where the Mackenzie River fans out into its huge delta. There they trapped abundant wildlife and lived off the amazing yield of the land, but the boisterous, burly French Canadian found the season long and difficult. His blue-eyed companion, the man with the Scandinavian accent, was a brooder, not a talker, and one summer with the silent, scowling Swede was enough. In early 1927 the two men bounced out of the bush and landed on the edge of the Pacific Ocean.

Vancouver was a bustling port city in the summertime, and the sound of commerce and the clink of glasses on the bar provided enough conviviality to encourage the French Canadian trapper to try a different endeavour with Johnson. The two adventurers looked into buying a boat with their cash, determined to make a living off the sea, but it was already too late in the season to make a go of fishing. Fate played her hand, and Johnson and his partner started a business providing wood and coal to merchants and business folk in the sea port.

It's not known for sure what happened in these early days of Albert Johnson's business life, but one thing is certain: some bad investments, money gone astray and dubious contacts in the fuel trade meant repeated, almost constant contact with the police. And authority was one thing Albert Johnson could not abide. By spring 1928, the strained partnership was dissolved and Albert Johnson was all too happy to leave the clang and clatter of the city to head for the solitude of the bush.

Johnson took increasing bitterness with him. When he headed north from Edmonton in the fall of 1928 with no companion, the trapper had pretty much shrugged off society. A deep grudge plagued him and he couldn't shake his feeling towards all law enforcement officers. Cops and red coats—those scarlet tunics of the RCMP were like a red flag to a raging bull. Johnson hated the Mounties with a deeply entrenched anger.

Albert Johnson, surviving alone in the North, fit the mould of solitary trapper the way a deer-hide moccasin hugs a foot. What he did between that first winter alone and the spring of 1931 can't be said for sure. Drought was upon the western prairies and the Great Depression was sending men, hungry for work, drifting across the country like tumbleweeds on the dustbowl prairies. They hopped trains, riding the rails both east and west. Maybe the thought of a wife and kids back home kept some of them south of the Sixtieth Parallel, but for the few who travelled northward, the sparsely populated Yukon and Northwest Territories was still wide open country. It was the last frontier, and provided a final hope of making a go of it.

It's all well and good if you choose to be alone, if the solitude suits you, but solitude can do funny things to your head. When the wind starts speaking and the trees call your name, cabin fever pure and simple might creep up on you. When cabin fever and bitterness mix, as they did in the case of Albert Johnson, it can be a deadly combination. When Albert Johnson went north the second time, he went wildly off the rails.

One can't recount the story of the Mad Trapper without reference to Arthur Nelson, either a name Johnson assumed or the man who became his first victim. Theories vary on whether Nelson and Johnson were one and the same. Both trapped in the same area, both had similar builds, both were men of few words who preferred their own company, and both, it turned out, spoke with a Scandinavian accent.

Roy Buttle, a trader at the Ross River Post, Yukon Territory, first encountered the man calling himself Arthur Nelson in late August 1927. Nelson had approached Buttle to ask for assistance building a boat to take him further into the bush. When the RCMP later tracked down information on Nelson, Buttle told them the trapper claimed to be from North Dakota. The man offered little personal information, but Buttle reported Nelson as "a highly intelligent fellow, good with words but using them sparingly."

At the time the RCMP began investigating Nelson's disappearance in 1931, reports of exchanges with him trickled into the RCMP from various traders and trappers between

Ross River Post and Mayo, Yukon. He had been in the area four seasons, always in possession of his 30-30 Savage rifle and a box or two of Dodd's Kidney Pills, a cure-all for sudden, unforeseen illnesses. Nelson swore this remedy would heal anything from head injuries to hangnails. A trader in Mayo said the pills and the Salvage rifle were Nelson's trademark—he'd lay the gun across his belly, reach into his pouch and pull out "the treatment."

Records at the Taylor & Drury Supply Warehouse in Mayo show a man calling himself Arthur Nelson selling marten skins for $680 in late August 1928. A cheque for that amount was cashed at the Bank of Montreal on August 30, 1928 and Nelson received, among lesser notes, a fifty dollar bill. While that may not seem significant now, a fifty dollar note was a small fortune then, and the serial number of the bill was dutifully recorded in the bank's large bill ledger.

The last sighting of what was believed to be Nelson was three years later on the McQuesten River, heading upstream to the Beaver River in early spring, after the onset of the Depression. Trapper Snoose Erikson reported to police a gruff exchange with Nelson just prior to his paddling north. Two months later Albert Johnson arrived in Fort McPherson, NWT on the Peel River, just north of the confluence of the Beaver and Peel. In his possession was a very familiar 30-30 Savage hunting rifle, the same fifty dollar note issued to Nelson back in 1928, and those infamous kidney pills he favoured so.

Now, truth be told, Nelson could have drowned, his abandoned camp discovered by Johnson who helped himself to the booty. Or Nelson could have been Johnson living all those years under an alias. However, given the history of the solitary Swede, it is just as possible Nelson was his first victim.

In a small settlement the arrival of a stranger is deemed an event and Albert Johnson's camp, three miles upstream from the settlement of Fort McPherson, caused a stir in the community. RCMP officer Constable Edgar (Spike) Millen, who'd been seven years in the North, was working out of the detachment of Arctic Red River, twenty-five miles as the crow flies east of Johnson's Peel River camp. As part of his regular patrols, Millen decided to pay the newcomer a call. He wanted to make sure the stranger wasn't up against a lifestyle he wasn't prepared for.

He found Johnson "short of outfit but not short of cash," and while he wasn't exactly forthcoming, Johnson did tell Millen he was planning to head up Rat River way, where trapping was good. Johnson's camp seemed woefully under-equipped. Milled noticed that Johnson wasn't outfitted to go anywhere, yet the trapper was talking about a voyage up the tough Rat River portage. When making small talk about some of the ill-prepared men he'd encountered in his time, Millen was interrupted by Johnson: "I don't like people sniffing around here. I want you to leave me be. Leave me alone."

"You'll need a licence," Millen told him, noting the scowl that passed across Johnson's face. "Can't trap without a licence."

Millen left Johnson's camp puzzled. The man had few supplies, but lots of cash. Not to mention he was mean and nasty. As Millen headed into Fort McPherson, determined to report his suspicions about the trapper to his superiors in Aklavik and Arctic Red River, he decided there was something strange about Johnson. Trouble was brewing.

The Northern Traders Ltd. and Hudson's Bay Company in Fort McPherson confirmed that on July 9, 1931, Johnson had picked up some outfitting gear, purchased a 16-gauge Iver

ALBERT JOHNSON

Johnson single-barrelled shotgun and twenty-five shells, bought a canoe from a native who was staying in the settlement, and headed up the Peel to the Husky River.

At the mouth of the Husky, trader and ex-RCMP officer Arthur Blake reported Johnson had passed by his post once, obviously looking

CONSTABLE EDGAR "SPIKE" MILLEN

for the mouth of the smaller Rat River. The second time Johnson went past Blake's cabin he ignored advice to back-track, raving instead about getting to the Rat by paddling up a small creek and making two portages.

"It seemed to me a crazy way to go with a loaded canoe but I wasn't about to argue," said Blake. "This was a man who'd rather hump his canoe over two groundswells than track, who am I to tell him different?"

Various people who spoke to Johnson report common traits. He was strong—five foot nine inches tall, with an average, solid build. He was confident in his bush skills, preferred his own company to anyone else's and he had a gruff and abrupt manner. In short, Johnson would rather not interact with fellow human beings. If he had to, he made sure the experience was so unpleasant that no one would make a second attempt at conversation.

Despite his anti-social tendencies, Albert Johnson knew how to survive in the bush. After contact with Blake, he headed

221

up the Rat and traversed a series of rapids so treacherous they were dubbed "Destruction City" because of the number of canoes they had consumed. Ten miles above these rapids, in autumn 1931, Albert Johnson constructed a cabin no bigger than an average pool table. Not only was it small, but the walls were dug down into the earth so that only the top three feet were exposed to the brutal elements of an arctic winter. The shack also commanded a view of the river from three sides. It was built like a bunker, and considering what was to come, a bunker it needed to be.

The first hint of trouble came to Spike Millen through a much-respected Dene named William Nerysoo on Christmas Day, 1931. He told the constable that Johnson had ripped apart his traps where their two lines crossed, even though "the wild white man" was the newcomer to traditional trapping territory of the Dene, not the other way round.

Because Millen's regular constable Roland Melville was in hospital at Aklavik, Millen called on Constable Alfred (Buns) King and Special Constable Joe Bernard to travel to Rat River. They were to check out Johnson, make sure his trapping licence was valid and question him about destroying the traps of the local natives.

Leaving from the Arctic Red River detachment on Saturday, December 26, 1931, the two men made the twenty-five-mile trip in two days, mushing through pitch-black darkness and freezing cold. The men approached Johnson's shack on Rat River at around ten o'clock in the morning. Smoke was coming from the chimney and it was obvious Johnson was hunkered down inside, although he didn't answer the shouts and knocks from King and Bernard. The two men spent nearly an hour at the cabin without any acknowledgement whatsoever from its occupant. The cabin was silent, breathing human life, but eerily silent.

"We'd better head out," said King to his colleague, and reluctantly they retraced the recently carved sled tracks and paw prints, deep in the blue-white snow, back down the Rat River. Instead of heading back, they would have to make the trek to Sub-District Headquarters in Aklavik. Their superior, Alexander Eames, would have to hear about the strange reception they had received from the man calling himself Albert Johnson.

Eames was also troubled. Johnson was in a very isolated spot. He'd holed up well, and access to his camp was difficult. Eames put two extra men on the job—Special Constable Lazarus Sittichiulis (in different accounts the name is spelled Sittichinlis but this is probably because of the translation of Indian names to English), an Indian RCMP officer as quick with a grin as he was with a gun, and Constable Robert McDowell, a four-year veteran of the force and a sled man of some note. The four officers, with two dog teams, headed back into the bush, intent on resolving the dilemma that had presented itself up the Rat River.

The winter of 1931–1932 was extremely cold and the men were frustrated by their efforts to contact Johnson. By the time they arrived at his cabin, the forty below weather was making tempers run thin. For the second time in less than a week, Constable Buns King approached the slouched shack. Before he could reach the door, a shot rang out. To the horror of his colleagues, King collapsed in the snow. Wounded but not dead, he wormed his way out of the range of fire. The RCMP pumped round after round into Albert Johnson's cabin but in the after-silence only the groans of agony from the gravely injured King pierced the frozen air. Lashing him to the lead sled, Millen and his men turned tail and fled, racing the clock to get King the medical aid he so desperately needed.

"He's probably dead inside that cabin," speculated Millen, with a backwards glance, but no one ventured near the cabin and no one knew how terribly wrong Spike Millen was. Johnson was far from dead.

On January 9, 1932, the RCMP were back at Rat River. King had lived—the bullet passed within an inch of his heart—but Inspector Eames' patience had worn thin. One of his men had been hurt, and the others were spending far too much time in freezing weather trying to flush the Swede like a rat from his hole. Nine men and a goodly amount of dynamite would quickly lay waste to the troublesome trapper.

Wrong again. The RCMP officers decided to storm the camp but as soon as they were over the bank Johnson commenced firing. A trapper named Knud Lang, recruited for his reputation of bravery, blasted the door off the cabin and claims he saw Johnson crouch below the earth firing two automatic pistols. The siege, including lobbing sticks of dynamite at the crude cabin, continued for fifteen hours to no avail. The Mad Trapper had stockpiles of ammunitions and he was not giving up the fight. The last round of dynamite, a four-pound bundle thrown by Lang, took out most of the shack. "We've got him," Inspector Eames cried.

Wrong again. Out of the blackened rubble came shots. A glaring torch intended to temporarily blind Johnson, who police presumed lay bleeding in the rubble, was blasted out of RCMP hands. Saving their own hides took priority and the party retreated.

Mid-winter, with temperatures hovering just below forty degrees, is miserable even for the heartiest northerner. The dogs were low on feed, the men exhausted. Eames decided to give everyone a break. They headed back to Aklavik on January 12, disheartened but determined to take out the madman who had such little regard for the law and even less for human life.

Two days later, on January 14, 1932, Spike Millen, the man who had chided Johnson about a trapper's licence the summer before on the banks of the Peel, was sent back to Rat River. He was part of a new posse of eight men led by Inspector Eames. The band included trapper Karl Garlund and the mighty Special Constable Sittichiulis. All were determined to succeed in the mission this time. In fact, news of the manhunt had reached Edmonton, and the antics of the Mad Trapper and his ability to elude the law had spread across the prairies like wildfire. With the Depression heavy upon them, people were eager to hear more tales of the elusive Mad Trapper of Rat River. Every man in the posse envisioned himself being the one to end the manhunt.

But Johnson was a slippery devil. For thirteen days the men visited old cabins and staked out his trap lines but no evidence was found proving that Johnson had recently been there. Despite fanning out and traversing the Rat River canyon clear up to the Bear River, Johnson and all his tracks and trappings seemed to have been obliterated by the constant wind and blowing snow.

On January 29, a portion of the original posse led by Millen found Johnson's secret camp in a thick patch of timber five miles from the mouth of a creek that empties into the Rat, a good mile north of the Barrier River. The four men surrounded the camp and, just as Millen was about to shout a warning, Johnson pierced him with his ice-blue eyes. His 30-30 pumped a hail of bullets and the RCMP returned fire. After what seemed an eternity there was silence. Johnson was down behind a log. There was no movement.

"I'm going to take him," said Millen to his partner Sergeant Riddell, who crouched beside him in the snow. "He's got to be dead."

"I'll cover you."

The two men cautiously descended the slope towards the spot where they believed Albert Johnson lay in a pool of blood. It was a fateful mistake. A shot rang out. "Get down," shouted Riddell, diving to the snow for cover. But it was too late.

Millen returned two shots before a bullet pierced his heart, instantly felling him. While Millen's comrades attended to him, trying desperately to stop the bleeding, the Mad Trapper scaled a cliff and escaped into the night woods. He was now, most certainly, a murderer.

By the time the men got Millen's body back to Aklavik, it was frozen solid, a grim reminder that, until he was stopped, Albert Johnson would continue to kill. Inspector Eames who knew the harsh countryside, the terrible winter conditions and the manpower amassed against Johnson, was astounded and somewhat awed that this man was still on the lam.

It's difficult to have respect for a killer, but Eames admitted a grudging admiration for the cunning of Albert Johnson. Outright shelling of the man hadn't brought him to his knees. Dynamite hadn't worked. A huge posse of some of the most experienced policemen hadn't worked. Sickened by the knowledge that Constable Millen was dead, Eames radioed Edmonton and urged famed bush pilot and World War I flying ace Wop May to take on the manhunt from the air. On February 7, 1932, for the first time in Canadian history, an aerial search was conducted for a fugitive. May buzzed the Barrier River valley and reported seeing the weighted snowshoe tracks of the Mad Trapper among the markings of a caribou herd.

Whether or not Johnson saw the bush plane is unknown, but something scared him. Against all odds, the desperate trapper

SEARCH PARTY FOR ALBERT JOHNSON

had crossed the 5000-foot Richardson Mountains that separate the Yukon from the Northwest Territories. When the RCMP descended, his Barrier River camp was cold and Johnson was, amazingly, on the west side of the mountains. He had bought himself time.

It wasn't until seven days later on February 14, that Wop May picked up Johnson's trail some eighteen miles up the Eagle River on the Yukon side. He had walked in tracks of caribou to elude aerial detection, travelling light, burrowing into the snow for sleep and surviving by his wits. But the Mounties knew they were at last closing in on their prey.

Six dog teams and eleven men—RCMP, ex-RCMP, trappers and woodsmen—convened fifteen miles from the mouth of the

Eagle River where they could follow Johnson's trail quite easily in the soft snow. The temperatures were slightly warmer and there was excitement and fear in the posse camp.

Just before noon on February 17, almost eight weeks since Inspector Eames had heard the first complaint against the surly

Swede, Albert Johnson was spotted trudging down the frozen river, 800 feet from the posse.

He saw the Mounties as he came around a bend in the river and made a wild dash for the bank but not before two of the posse, RCMP Staff Sergeant Earl Heresy and trapper Joseph

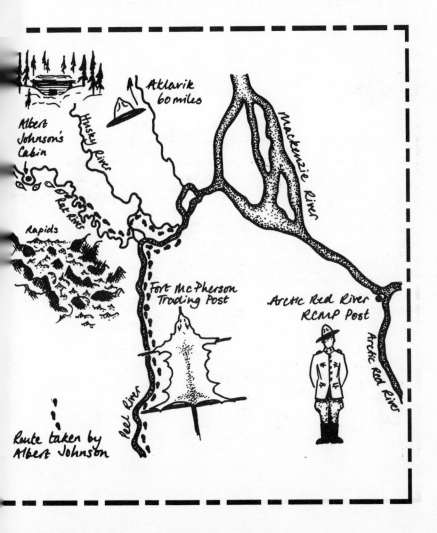

Verve, fired their rifles at the frantic figure. Johnson returned fire and a raging gun battle took place in the middle of a desolate landscape.

"I'm hit!" shouted Heresy but his words were lost to a burble of blood streaming from his mouth. He had taken bullets in the knee, elbow and chest and one of his lungs was punctured. Another man felled by Albert Johnson.

It seemed Johnson could not die. Totally surrounded by men on the wide expanse of river ice, he was still getting shots away. Three more shots were fired from his 30-30 before the Mad Trapper was silenced at last.

It took seventeen bullets to bring the man down. Seventeen bullets ended the forty-eight-day manhunt that covered 150 miles of arctic ice and fascinated the world in 1931–32. And in the wake of his wild rampage in the Canadian Arctic, Albert Johnson left one, possibly two men dead and two others seriously wounded. There was no motive established for these killings. When at last Albert Johnson died at 12:10 p.m. on February 17, 1932, on the frozen Eagle River, his icy blue eyes were wide open, and his lips twisted into a grotesque smile.